Barbecue

R&R PUBLICATIONS MARKETING PTY LTD

Published by
R&R Publications Marketing Pty Ltd
ABN 78 348 105 138

PO Box 254, Carlton North,
Victoria 3054 Australia
PHONE: (61 3) 9381 2199
FAX: (61 3) 9381 2689
E-MAIL: info@randrpublications.com.au
WEBSITE: www.randrpublications.com.au
AUSTRALIA-WIDE TOLL-FREE: 1800 063 296

© Anthony Carroll 2006

Barbecue – Collectors Edition

PUBLISHER: Anthony Carroll
PRODUCTION MANAGER: Neil Hargreaves
GRAPHIC DESIGNER: Elain Wei Voon Loh
FOOD EDITOR: Neil Hargreaves
FOOD PHOTOGRAPHY: Brent Parker Jones, R&R Photstudio
FOOD STYLISTS: Neil Hargreaves, Lee Blaylock
PROOFREADER: Sandra Goldbloom Zurbo

ISBN 978-1-74022-603-5

Printed December 2007
Computer Typeset in
ITC Avant Garde Gothic
Printed in China

Contents

Introduction

What was once a crude way of cooking freshly killed game over a fire has evolved into a fabulous art form in its own right. Innovations in barbecuing have created nuances in the taste of meat, fish and seafood, as well as fruit and vegetables that have found their home in even the finest eateries in Europe.

HISTORY

Delving into the history books reveals that early explorers noted the way in which indigenous people would dry meat and fish on a frame fashioned from green saplings and placed over a smouldering fire.

Spaniards dubbed this makeshift grill *barbacoa*, while French settlers, who slowly roasted whole animals top to tail, coined the term, *barbe-a-queue*. The sophisticated variations that have resulted from this simple but brilliant technique have delighted generations. Fire, often a destructive force, has a creative power in cooking; its wispy by-product, smoke, adds a whole new dimension to the pleasures of the palate.

For the sake of precision, barbecuing is distinguished from grilling and smoking in that it imparts a distinct smoky flavor to food. Experimenting with wonderful variations to all three methods of cooking, or even applying a novel seasoning to spice it up, has produced proud cooks throughout the world who boast that they have the finest fare.

Getting Started

This book has been designed to provide you with an overview of cooking on your barbecue and, where necessary, indepth descriptions of methods to help you achieve exact results.

The first section deals with choosing the right tools. Whether for a simple meal or a lavish affair, selecting the right equipment is essential; knowing how to use it to its maximum effectiveness is even more so. The choice of equipment can significantly alter cooking times, hands-on labor and, most importantly, the outcome of your food. For example, did you know that lava rock in gas grills is almost impossible to clean effectively and if it has a coating of burnt-on grease it can give food an unpleasant flavor? This sort of know-how can only come from experts in the field, and we are committed to passing it onto you.

The second section is concerned with the fuels that power your barbecue. From hardwoods to self-lighting briquettes, the equipment you use and the taste you are trying to achieve with your chosen method will influence your choice of fuel. To give you an idea of what is at stake, you will inevitably develop a bias towards hardwood chunks of hickory, alder, mesquite or applewood if you want to achieve an unmistakable smoky flavor in your cuisine. Take old-fashioned techniques and apply them to a contemporary setting to get the best of both worlds–centuries-old traditions coupled with modern conveniences.

The third section brings together your newly acquired knowledge of tools, equipment and fuel to guide you in preparing the barbecue or grill for optimum performance. Whether you use the direct-heat or indirect-heat method depends on the type of food you are cooking and the look you want to create. To seal in natural juices, for example, opt for the direct-heat method, which sears your meat with a characteristic grilled appearance.

Combine your choice of cooking technique with dry spice rubs, sauces or marinades – taste combinations are endless.

You will be thrilled by what a marinade can do to your meat — tenderise its flesh and charge it with extravagant flavors. Whether a tangy honey and chili combination or a smooth red wine and garlic marinade, you will find expert tips here on how to handle tougher cuts and how to prevent your marinated meats from being charred on the barbecue.

Whether using commercial preparations or homemade concoctions, there is enough variety in this book to adapt to family meals or special occasions. We have assigned chapters to beef and veal, lamb, pork, chicken, seafood, vegetables and bread for quick reference.

Equipment

The world of outdoor cooking has come a long way since the days of throwing a few sausages and steaks onto a hotplate straddled over an open fire. Significant advances in the design of backyard cookers now enable you to produce exquisite meals that you never thought possible.

Listed here are basic grill shapes and types and other equipment you may find useful for barbecuing and grilling and, in some cases, for cooking over a campfire. Recipes in this book were tested and cooked perfectly on a 4 jet gas barbecue.

Other equipment, such as a drip pan and an instant-read thermometer (neither of which is very expensive), are essential for more sophisticated recipes. For simpler fare, little equipment is needed; in most cases standard kitchenware can be used, but use on and around the grill is hard on tools not designed for that use. Although you do not have to purchase a great deal of equipment to enjoy grilling, you may find it beneficial to have some of these items for your outdoor cooking.

There are many and varied barbecue models available today. It is very important to carefully read the manufacturer's instructions that come with each model.

KETTLE-SHAPED GRILLS

The kettle-shaped grill revolutionised outdoor cooking. The sophisticated design eliminated the need to control heat by lowering and raising the grill, and saved the cook from constant battles with flare-ups and uneven heat. The kettle-shaped grill is designed for cooking with the lid closed. Carefully placed vents in the top and bottom provide adequate airflow to keep the fire going and completely eliminate flare-ups. Thus, searing over a very hot fire can easily be accomplished without burning the food. If the coals are moved to each side of the kettle and a drip pan positioned in the centre, food can also be cooked more slowly; this is the indirect-heat method of cooking.

There are two main drawbacks to the kettle-shaped grill. First, the lid is not hinged, which causes some inconvenience every time you open and close it. Second, the grill position is not adjustable; if the food is not quite ready but the fire is dying out, it's not possible to move the food closer to the coals to finish the job, which leaves you with two options neither of which is my satisfactory: finish under your kitchen griller or remove the food and rebuild the fire.

GAS GRILLS

The most recent step forward in the high-tech world of outdoor cooking is the introduction of a new generation of gas grills with sophisticated heat circulation and control. You'll find versions that have either lava rock or porcelain-coated metal bars. Both serve the same function — they evenly emanate heat from the gas burners below them and vapourise drippings from the food above, giving the food that distinct grilled flavor. In time, a difference between the two versions becomes evident. The lava rocks are nearly impossible to clean effectively; the layers of burnt grease give food an unpleasant flavor. The porcelain-coated bars are easily removed for cleaning and are dishwasher-safe.

Probably the greatest asset gas grills offer is the ability to control cooking temperatures. Beefeater Barbecues have units with two, three or four horizontal gas burners, that allow you to regulate the heat to the desired temperature. By experimenting a bit, you will find the gas grill to be just as accurate and responsive as your kitchen oven.

To some, cooking on a gas grill just doesn't seem like traditional outdoor cooking. How can food cooked over a gas grill even begin to taste as good as food cooked over a mesquite grill laden with applewood chips? This is a legitimate objection, but it is primarily emotional and romantic. The truth of the matter is that a gas grill is as good as the person cooking on it. Memorable and exceptional food can be produced on a gas grill — food that is just as good or better than fare from a charcoal grill. You just have to learn how to use a gas grill to produce the desired effects.

OPEN GRILLS

Some recipes in this chapter were developed for use with a covered grill, but you can use them with your open grill if you improvise a lid. Try using a large cooking pot or the lid of an electric skillet to cover the food. Or make a foil tent.

Open grills are not as easy to use as hooded grills, but they are often less expensive. Since they don't have a lid, you are very likely to experience flare-ups during cooking. The best way to handle this is to use an open grill to cook only foods that don't have an oil-based marinade or foods that are low in fat, such as fish and poultry. You can't effectively use the indirect-heat method of cooking when using an open grill because most of the heat simply wafts into the air. Keep a spray bottle of water handy to control flare-ups.

INDOOR GRILLS

Although this book was developed for cooking outdoors, most of the grilling recipes can be adapted for use on an indoor grill or if you don't have one, then on the stovetop or in the oven.

The most current indoor grills can be incorporated into the stovetop or set up on kitchen benches, thereby providing a year-round grilling appliance. Both electric and gas models are available. Whatever style of indoor grill you choose be sure it is correctly installed and that proper ventilation is maintained. Check the manufacturer's instructions for recipe adaptation methods, especially regarding cooking with marinades and the use of oil to prepare the grill. Oil sprays are convenient for oiling indoor electric grills and cast iron griddle plates or pans. Do not use on outdoor barbecues. There is a danger of flare–ups and accidentally leaving the spray container on the side of the barbecue.

DRIP PAN

A drip pan is essential for the indirect-heat method of cooking. Your best bet is to purchase a disposable aluminium pan — a 5–75mm deep rectangle — and dispose of it measure after each use.

GRILL BRUSH

This inexpensive tool is a must for proper grill care. Brush grill before oiling, and after cooking while the grill is still hot to remove any food particles or burned-on grease. If you follow this procedure consistently, you won't have to wash the grill with cleanser, which ruins the seasoning.

HINGED WIRE BASKET

These baskets hold fish fillets, hamburger patties or bread between two grills secured by a latch. Simply place the food inside the basket and place the basket over the heat. When one side is done, flip it over. It is necessary to lightly oil the basket before placing food inside.

INSTANT-READ THERMOMETER

Old-style thermometers take too long to work to provide accurate cooking temperatures for grilled foods. The instant-read versions provide an accurate picture of the progress within 5 seconds of insertion.

ROAST RACKS

Made of aluminium or stainless steel, V-shaped roast racks do an excellent job holding large pieces of meat or poultry together as they cook. If you use one while cooking with indirect heat, you don't need to turn the meat at all; it cooks evenly on all sides.

SKEWERS

Metal and bamboo are common skewer materials. Metal skewers never burn up, but you do have to wash them. You need to soak bamboo skewers in water for 15–30 minutes before use to prevent them from burning. If you are fortunate enough to have rosemary growing nearby, try using these branches for skewers. Remove the leaves and soak the branches in water for 30 minutes. They imbue the skewered food with a pungent flavor.

SPATULA

Take the time to find an offset stainless steel spatula with a blade 5–6 in/ 12.5–15cm long — the kind professional chefs use. The advantage of the long blade is that it will slide under most chops and fish fillets completely which means they won't tear or stick when being flipped over. Stainless steel will never rust and is easy to care for.

SPRAY BOTTLE

With the advent of kettles and gas grills, there aren't many fire flare-ups any more. But always keep a spray bottle filled with water next to your grill, just in case of an emergency.

TONGS

Tongs are probably the most useful and versatile grill tool that you can buy. Use a pair that is at least 11¾ in/30cm long and spring-loaded. It's not a bad idea to have two pairs, one to move hot charcoal around and one to use with food. (Of course, you can get by with one pair — you will just have to keep wiping it off every time you use it to move charcoal.)

Fuels

Shopping for fuel in a well-stocked market can be quite a confusing experience. Many different fuels now compete with traditional charcoal briquettes. Mesquite charcoal, hardwood charcoals, hardwood-flavored charcoals, self-lighting briquettes and a number of different types of smoke-creating hardwood chips, chunks and sawdust all crowd the shelf. They all work well in the right situation. You must judge what will work best for you.

WOODS

Use oak, hickory, cherry, apple, mesquite or alder as a wood for outdoor cooking. Be aware, however, that, although a wood-burning barbecue is romantic, it doesn't make much sense. Wood takes a considerable time to burn down to useable coals and wood coals don't last as long as charcoal briquettes or hardwood charcoal. With wood you end up waiting twice as long to cook, and then your fire goes out sooner. Instead of using these woods as your major fuel source, use the smaller pieces as kindling and cut the remainder into 1 in/25mm chunks to add a smoky complement to your fire. Never use a softwood for smoking or as a fuel; the thick resins produce a distinctly unpleasant aftertaste. Be careful about burning scrap wood. Pressure-treated timber (the type of wood used in outdoor construction), for instance, contains chemicals that can be toxic.

APPLEWOOD

Applewood provides a subtle smoky flavor that is not nearly as pronounced as that of mesquite, oak or hickory. It imparts a slightly sweet but dense smoky flavor, that is marvellous with poultry and ham.

HARDWOOD CHUNKS AND SAWDUST

Food cooked over hardwood has a distinctive smoky flavor. Hickory, alder, mesquite and applewood are the most popular and most widely available woods.

If you use a gas grill, hardwood chips work better than chunks. Select pieces ⅛–1 in/1–25mm thick and soak them in water for at least 30 minutes before you use them. Place an old aluminium pie pan over the gas heating elements toward the back corner of your grill before you turn it on, and place the water-soaked chips in the pan. As the grill heats up, the chips will begin to smoulder. If you cook with high heat, you may experience flare-ups from the chips so have your spray bottle ready. The only limitation of this method is that the chips tend to burn quickly. You'll have to monitor their progress and replenish the chips as necessary, but don't put too many on at once or you will extinguish your fire.

For the gas grill, hardwood sawdust works as well or better than hardwood chips. Easy to ignite, sawdust provides a consistent, flavorful smoke. To use, place sawdust in an old pie pan and place directly on top of lava rocks or flavoriser bars. Turn gas burners to high until sawdust just blackens and begins to smoulder. Immediately turn off burner underneath pan. Replenish sawdust as needed. Hardwood sawdust is available at timber yards, barbecue supplies stores and specialty cookware stores.

MESQUITE

Mesquite is a scrub hardwood tree that grows wild in the arid plains of the southwest of America and in Mexico and is available at barbecue supplies stores.

Sweeter and more delicate than hickory, mesquite is a perfect complement to richly flavored meats such as beef and lamb, as well as to duck.

FRESH HERBS AND CITRUS RINDS

Thyme, bay leaves, rosemary, oregano and marjoram are particularly well suited to flavoring your fire.

Chose one type of herb, moisten it with water (for an added taste treat, use wine or liquor to moisten it), and toss it onto the coals right before you put food on the grill. Try lemon, orange or lime rinds as well. Add them one at a time, with or without a complementary fresh herb. Be careful not to directly inhale the fumes of burning herbs or fruit rinds; they can be rather overpowering.

Fire Starting

Whatever method you use, allow about 30–45 minutes for your fire to start. The idea is to start the fire in your grill, not in your house. When you use a gas barbecue it will only take a few minutes to attain the correct temperature.

KINDLING

Starting a fire with kindling is probably the most individual and ritual-laden method. Although each fire starter has a unique style, the basic method is to start with a few sheets of newspaper and crumple them loosely or twist them into logs. Place these logs in the bottom of your grill, and then place a handful of dry kindling on top. Place five or six briquettes on top of the kindling. Light the newspaper.

If the briquettes do not light, add more newspaper and kindling until they do. Once the briquettes are alight add more briquettes on top until you have a fire of the desired size. Everyone seems to have their own ratio of newspaper to kindling to briquettes. Just do what works for you.

ELECTRIC STARTER

Electricity is certainly the easiest and most foolproof means of starting a fire. Check the manufacturer's recommendations for starting a fire with an electric starter in your grill. In most cases, the instructions tell you to arrange your briquettes in a pile on top of the starter, plug it in and let it go to work. In about 10 minutes, your briquettes should be started. Don't leave your starter in any longer, or the heating element will be damaged by lengthy exposure to high heat. The only disadvantage to this fire-starting method is that you need to be near an electrical connection.

CHARCOAL CHIMNEY

The simplicity and ease of charcoal chimneys make them a wonder to watch. A charcoal chimney is nothing more than an open-ended, sheet-metal cylinder vented at the lower end, with a grate about 4 in/10cm from the bottom to set the charcoal briquettes on. To use, simply crumple several sheets of newspaper and place them under the grate. Fill the chimney with charcoal briquettes, and place in the bottom of the grill and light the paper. In about 10 minutes the briquettes will begin to smoulder. Once all the briquettes are well ignited, pour them out of the chimney into the bottom of your grill.

A charcoal chimney is also the answer when you will be using your grill for several hours and don't want to replenish your fire with raw charcoal briquettes because of the fumes they emit when they just start to burn.

Simply set the chimney on an old pie pan on a concrete surface and light more charcoal. When the briquettes are ready, pour them onto your existing fire.

You can make your own charcoal chimney by cutting the top and bottom off a coffee or food can and making a vent in the bottom with a can opener. If you buy a ready-made chimney, you will find that it is inexpensive and has the added benefits of a wooden handle and a grate to set the charcoal on.

HOW MUCH FIRE?

When determining the size of your fire, first imagine the cooking surface that the food requires. Spread the briquettes out on a single layer to cover an area about 1 in/25mm past the edges that you have imagined. Now add about half again as much charcoal and you should have, enough for an hour's worth of fire. Usually, 30–40 briquettes are sufficient to cook food for four people. If you are making a fire for slow cooking using the indirect-heat method, use about 25 briquettes on each side of the grill. Plan on adding 8–10 briquettes to each side for every hour of additional cooking time.

WHEN IS THE FIRE READY?

It usually takes between 30 and 45 minutes for a fire to be ready for cooking. Never cook over a fire until the briquettes are covered with a light ash and are no longer flaming. Cooking over a direct flame burns the outside of your food and leaves the inside raw. Your hand is probably the best judge of when a fire is ready.

Hold your hand flat over the fire at grill height. You will be able to hold your hand over a very hot fire for about 2 seconds. If the fire is hot, you can hold your hand above it for 3–4 seconds. If you can hold it any longer than that, you have let the fire die down too much.

Add more briquettes and let it build up again. A very hot fire is ideal for the direct-heat method of cooking; a medium to hot fire is desirable for the indirect-heat method. Once your fire is ready, carefully add hardwood chips or fresh herbs. Put the grill in place and let it heat up for 4–5 minutes before putting on food.

PREPARING THE GRILL

Always arrange the fire so that there are areas of the grill with no fire under them. If some of your food is done sooner than others, move it to these cooler spots to keep finished food warm while the remainder of the meal cooks. Brush the grill lightly with oil right after you put it in place over the fire. To do this, moisten a paper towel with oil. Using tongs held in a fireproof mitt-clad hand, rub the oil from the towel onto the grill. This will help prevent food from sticking to the grill and will also keep the grill seasoned.

Always keep the grill clean. The best method is to quickly brush the excess food off with a grill brush immediately after you finish cooking. This way the remaining fire will burn off any lingering bits and you won't have to resort to soap and water, which would ruin the seasoning of the grill surface. If you do not have a grill brush use a crumpled wad of aluminium foil held with tongs.

Have all your grill tools ready and available before you light your fire. Tongs, mitts and spray bottle are particularly important to have at your fingertips. Have extra charcoal available. There is nothing more frustrating than discovering that your fire is dying before dinner is ready and there is no more charcoal.

OUTDOOR COOKING METHODS

With the advent of covered grills, a whole new world of barbecuing opened up. Foods can now be slowly roasted over indirect heat so that they become tender and stay moist during cooking. Whether to use indirect-heat cooking or traditional grilling over direct heat depends on the type of food to be cooked and the result desired.

DIRECT-HEAT METHOD

Use the direct-heat cooking method to sear foods to seal in their natural juices and to give the characteristic grilled look. Foods that are low in fat, such as poultry and fish, and foods that don't take very long to cook are ideal choices for this method. Hamburgers, chops, vegetables, skewered items and fish fillets all fall within this category.

If using charcoal, start your fire and, after 30–45 minutes, when the coals have a light grey ash covering, spread them out one briquette deep so that you have an even cooking source.

Place your grill over the coals and let it heat up for 4–5 minutes.

If you are using pre-soaked hardwood chips or chunks or moistened fresh herbs, spread them out over the coals before placing food on the grill. The wood will immediately begin to smoulder. Now you're ready to cook. When using a kettle-shaped grill, keep the lid closed for the duration of cooking; regulate the heat by adjusting the upper and lower vents. The beauty of this system is the total lack of flare-ups, even though the food is cooking at a very high temperature and fat is dripping onto the coals. The fat vaporizes as it hits the coals, imparting a desirable smoky flavor to the food, but the fat doesn't have enough oxygen to ignite into an undesirable flame.

Heat circulation in the kettle-shaped grill is excellent, cooking the food on top as well as on bottom. You still need to flip the food over due to the short cooking time, but it does cook faster and more evenly inside a kettle. So it is very important that the lid stays closed except when you need to baste, add coals, check the food or turn it over.

Otherwise, leave the grill alone and let it cook.

If you are using a gas grill, turn all three burners to high and close the lid. Your grill should be sufficiently hot to cook on in about 10 minutes. Depending on the food being cooked and the desired effect, you can leave the temperature on high while cooking or turn down one or more burners. There is a nearly immediate response to the burner temperature controls, so experiment to find the exact temperature you want.

DIRECT 2 ZONE HEATING METHOD

Preparing the barbecue for 2 Zone Direct Heat gives greater control for cooking food. It creates a hot to very hot area for searing the food and a moderately hot area for cooking through to desired readiness. An outer third area may be created for keeping cooked food warm.

CHARCOAL BARBECUE

When coals are ready, pile 2 layers of coals to the left half of the area and I row to the right half. Put the grill rack in place and allow 4–5 minutes for the rack to heat. If you wish to have a third zone leave the outer right edge without coals.

GAS BARBECUE

Set the burners on the left side to high and the right side burners to medium to create 2 heat zones. To create a third zone leave the far right burner off.

INDIRECT-HEAT METHOD

The indirect-heat method of cooking is where recent advances in grill designs have yielded the most spectacular results. You can now cook foods on the grill that were unimaginable ten years ago. Whole prime ribs, turkeys and chickens will cook beautifully without even needing to be turned over. Foods traditionally braised slowly in the oven with plenty of cooking liquid, such as veal breasts and pheasant, can now be done outdoors.

The reason is that the food is placed over a drip pan with no direct heat under it. All the heat circulates around the food, in much the same way as it does in a convection oven. Thus, you won't need to turn over a large roast, for example, because it cooks just as fast on top as it does underneath. (You probably will want to turn smaller cuts to obtain equal colorations and grill marks.)

Another advantage of this method is the absence of the sometimes difficult-to-handle rotisserie. It simply isn't needed any more.

If you are using a charcoal grill, prepare your coals as per the Direct-Heat Method. When they are covered with a light grey ash, separate them into two piles on each side of the kettle. Place a disposable aluminium drip pan between the piles. If you are using pre-soaked hardwood chips or chunks or moistened fresh herbs, add them to the piles now. Put the grill in place and allow it to heat up for 4–5 minutes before positioning the food on the grill directly over the drip pan.

If you want to sear the food first, simply place the food directly over one side of the coals until it is browned, and then move it over the drip pan. Close the lid and regulate the temperature by adjusting the upper and lower vents. Since the indirect-heat cooking method often takes several hours, you will occasionally need to add more briquettes.

If you are using a gas grill, pre-heat the grill with all three burners on high. The grill should be hot in about 10 minutes. Turn off the centre burner and carefully position the disposable aluminium drip pan over it.

Place the oiled grill in position and turn up the grill heat for 4–5 minutes. Place the food directly over the drip pan. Close the lid and let the food cook. Regulate the temperature by adjusting the two outer burners; leave the centre burner off. For recipes calling for a temperature of 356°–392°F/180°–200°C, turn the burners to medium. For recipes calling for 302°–320°F/150°–160°C turn both burners to low.

If you want a smoky flavor, see page 10 for a discussion of using hardwood chips in a gas grill. If you are using moistened fresh herbs, throw them directly onto the outside porcelain bars, then close the lid. Remember that these grills are designed to operate most effectively when the lid is closed. Open the lid only to check on or to baste the food or to add more chips or herbs.

Barbecue
with smoke...

- Use the natural ingredients from around you to embellish the smoky flavors of your barbecue foods.

- Sprigs of fresh herbs, wood chips and citrus rinds can all be soaked in either wine or water, then added to the coals just before you start to cook.

- You will not only scent the food, you will fill the cooking environment with wonderful aromas.

makes 24 | Bruschetta

PREPARATION 30 mins   COOKING 10 mins

¾ cup extra virgin olive oil

1 tablespoon freshly crushed garlic

2 ciabatta or baguette loaves

1 cup chunky salsa dip

shaved Parmesan cheese

PREPARATION

1 Mix the oil and garlic together, stand for 30 minutes to infuse. Cut the bread into ¾ in/15mm thick slices at an angle. Brush both sides with garlic oil. Tip the salsa into a small skillet.

AT THE BARBECUE

1 Prepare the barbecue for direct heat, medium high. Place the bread onto the heated grill bars or grill plate and toast both sides. Place the skillet of salsa at the side to warm up.

2 Remove toasted bread and brush lightly with extra garlic oil. Spoon the warm salsa thickly onto the toast and top with Parmesan shavings. Serve immediately.

Apricot, Bacon and Banana Bites

serves 4

Apricot, Bacon and Banana Bites

PREPARATION 5 mins   COOKING 10 mins

3 large firm bananas, peeled

4 strips bacon

¾ cup apricot marinade

(see page 169)

wooden cocktail sticks,

soaked for 30 minutes

PREPARATION

1 Cut bananas into 1½ in/35mm slices at an angle. Cut bacon into 4 in/10cm long strips. Wrap a strip of bacon around each banana piece, secure with a cocktail stick. Place on a tray and brush with the marinade.

AT THE BARBECUE

1 Prepare barbecue for medium direct heat.Oil the grill bars or grill plate. When ready, arrange the bananas in rows. Cook for 10 minutes or until bacon is cooked, brushing with extra marinade and turning frequently with tongs.

Nachos

serves 4

Nachos

PREPARATION 2 mins   COOKING 12 mins

8 oz/230g packet plain
corn chips

1 cup chunky tomato relish
(see page 181)

3 scallions, finely chopped
(optional)

300g guacamole-style dip

2 cups grated Cheddar
cheese

chili sauce of choice

PREPARATION

1 Place the corn chips onto 2 lightly greased heatproof platters, pizza trays or shallow baking tray. Mix the salsa dip and chopped scallions together.

AT THE BARBECUE

1 Have the barbecue ready for hot indirect cooking. Drop dollops of salsa mixture at intervals over the corn chips, then dollops of guacamole dip in the spaces. Top with grated cheese.

2 Place on the barbecue over indirect heat, cover with lid or hood and cook for 10–12 minutes or until the cheese is melted and bubbly. If needed, improvise a hood by placing an overturned baking dish over the platter. Serve immediately. The nachos are taken direct from the platter.

Lemon Pepper Chicken Sticks

serves 4

Lemon Pepper Chicken Sticks

PREPARATION 1 hr 35 mins   COOKING 10–12 mins

1 lb/500g ground chicken meat

½ cup breadcrumbs

1 medium onion, peeled

½ teaspoon salt

2 tablespoons chopped
fresh parsley

½ teaspoon lemon pepper

2 tablespoons lemon juice

oil for brushing

20 mini satay sticks, soaked in
water for 30 minutes

PREPARATION

1 Place the chicken in a bowl. Add the breadcrumbs. Using fine side of grater, grate the onion over the breadcrumbs to catch the juice. Add remaining ingredients except oil. Mix and knead well with hand to combine and make the chicken fine in grain. Stand for 15 minutes.

2 With wet hands take a portion of chicken and mould around the stick to a 1½ in/35mm length. Arrange on an oiled tray, cover and refrigerate for 1 hour.

AT THE BARBECUE

1 Prepare barbecue for medium-hot direct-heat cooking. Oil the grill and place the chicken sticks on. Cook for 10–12 minutes, or until cooked through, turning frequently. Serve hot.

Sweet Chili Shrimp Skewers

serves 4

Sweet Chili Shrimp Skewers

PREPARATION 1 hr 30 mins   COOKING 6–8 mins

2 lb/1kg medium-sized green jumbo shrimp

½ cup sweet chili sauce

mixed salad greens for serving

8 bamboo skewers, soaked in water for 30 minutes

PREPARATION

1 Shell the shrimp, leaving the tails on. Devein the shrimp. Place in a ceramic dish and pour over the sauce. Toss to coat all shrimp, cover and marinate in the refrigerator for 1 hour or more. Thread 3 shrimp through 2 sides onto each skewer.

AT THE BARBECUE

1 Prepare barbecue for medium-high direct cooking. Place the skewered shrimp on it. Cook for 2–3 minutes each side, brushing with marinade as they cook. When cooked they will turn pink.

Barbecued Cheese Fondue

serves 10–12

Barbecued Cheese Fondue

PREPARATION 2 mins COOKING 12 mins

2 cups béchamel sauce

10½ oz/300g Swiss cheese or mild Cheddar cheese cut into small cubes

½ cup white wine, warmed

1 loaf country style bread cut into 1 in/25mm cubes

PREPARATION

1 Select a suitable heatproof ceramic or earthenware bowl. Assemble the ingredients and utensils, including a wooden spoon and fondue forks or dinner forks. Take all to barbecue area.

AT THE BARBECUE

1 Place the fondue bowl on hot grill bars or grill plate to warm up. Pour in the béchamel sauce and heat, stirring occasionally until warm. Move the bowl to the side of the barbecue over milder heat or elevate onto a wire rack.

2 Commence adding cheese, stirring gently with a wooden spoon as it melts. Continue to add cheese and stirring until all cheese is added. Stir in some of the white wine until a nice coating consistency is achieved.

3 Move bowl to edge of the barbecue over mild heat. Invite guests to spear bread cube onto a fork and dip into the fondue. If necessary, thin down fondue with a little warmed white wine.

Apricot and Sausage Kebabs

makes 20

Apricot and Sausage Kebabs

PREPARATION 20 mins   COOKING 8–10 mins

5 thin pork sausages

4 oz/125g dried apricots, soaked

¾ cup apricot marinade (see page 169)

20 mini bamboo satay sticks, soaked in water for 30 minutes

PREPARATION

1 Par-grill the sausages carefully, turning frequently so they remain straight. Remove and allow to cool. When cold, cut each into 4 even pieces. Thread lengthwise onto the soaked satay skewers alternating with apricot.

AT THE BARBECUE

1 Prepare barbecue for medium-high direct cooking. Brush the kebabs with marinade and cook turning frequently and brushing with extra marinade for about 8–10 minutes or until cooked and well glazed. Serve immediately as finger food.

Plum-Glazed Chipolatas in a Basket

serves 4

Plum-Glazed Chipolatas in a Basket

PREPARATION 12 mins   COOKING 12 mins

2 lb/1kg chipolata sausages

½ cup sweet plum marinade
(see page 187)

1 bread basket

PREPARATION

1 Leave sausages in links, place in a skillet with water to just cover. Bring slowly to a simmer then remove from heat, cover and stand until sausages are firm. Drain well, separate sausages and refrigerate in a sealed container until needed. (May be done the night before.)

AT THE BARBECUE

1 Heat grill bars or grill plate using direct heat to medium high. Pour the marinade into a small skillet and place on the grill to heat. Remove to the side when heated.

2 Place a sheet of baking paper over grill bars or plate and arrange sausages in rows. Working left to right, cook sausages, brushing with marinade and turning frequently until cooked and well glazed.

3 Transfer sausages to heated bread basket. Place on a platter with extra marinade served separately. Provide cocktail picks for serving. Invite guests to partake of the bread basket as it empties.

Barbecued Stuffed Mushrooms

serves 12

Barbecued Stuffed Mushrooms

PREPARATION 16 mins   COOKING 8–10 mins

12 medium-sized mushrooms
about 1½–2 in/4–5cm in
diameter

3 strips bacon, rind removed,
and chopped

2 tablespoons fresh
breadcrumbs

3 tablespoons chunky tomato
relish (see page 181)

2 tablespoons finely chopped
fresh parsley

feta cheese, crumbed

PREPARATION

1 Remove the stems from the mushrooms,
trim off end of stem and finely chop the stems.

2 Heat a skillet, add bacon and cook until
the fat runs. Add the mushroom stems and
continue to cook the bacon and stems. Stir
in the breadcrumbs, salsa and parsley flakes.
Remove from heat and set aside.

3 Remove the skin from the mushrooms
and brush mushrooms with olive oil. Stuff the
mushroom caps with the stuffing. Place on a
tray. Sprinkle each mushroom with crumbled
feta, pressing gently on. Take to barbecue.

AT THE BARBECUE

1 Place mushrooms onto greased grill bars
over direct hot heat with hood down and cook
for 8–10 minutes. If barbecue has no hood or lid,
improvise by inverting a baking dish over the
mushrooms so the cheese will melt.

Barbecued Mussels with Chili Lime Dressing

serves 4

Barbecued Mussels with Chili Lime Dressing

PREPARATION 10 mins   COOKING 4 mins

about 4 dozen fresh green-lipped mussels in the shell

fresh chives for garnish

CHILI LIME DRESSING

1 clove garlic, crushed and finely chopped

¼ cup fresh lime juice

1 tablespoon Thai fish sauce

½ teaspoon prepared minced chili

½ teaspoon brown sugar

PREPARATION

1   Debeard mussels.

AT THE BARBECUE

1   Lay over barbecue hotplate. Cook until mussels open, covering if you have a lidded barbecue.

2   Discard any that do not open. Break off and discard top shell.

3   Arrange mussels on a platter and drizzle dressing over them. Garnish with chives.

4   For the chili lime dressing, mix garlic, lime juice, fish sauce, chili and brown sugar together.

Quick Sesame Chicken Wings

PREPARATION 1 hr 5 mins   COOKING 20 mins

4 lb/2kg chicken wings, tips removed
½ cup honey
3 tablespoons light soy sauce
2 tablespoons sherry
½ teaspoon fresh ginger, minced
½ teapoon fresh garlic, minced
3 tablespoons sesame seeds, toasted

PREPARATION

1 Combine honey, soy sauce,sherry, ginger and garlic together. Stir together to make marinade.

2 Place wings in a large container. Cover with marinade for 1 hour in the refrigerator.

3 Place half the wings in a microwave-safe dish and microwave for 7 minutes on high. Remove and microwave the remainder.

AT THE BARBECUE

1 Heat the barbecue until hot. Place a wire cake-rack over the grill bars and place the wings on the rack. Brush with marinade left in the bow. Turn and brush the wings frequently for 6 minutes until brown and crisp. While wings are crisping, spread sesame seeds on a foil tray and place on the barbecue. Shake occasionally as they toast. Sprinkle over the chicken wings and serve.

Lemon Pepper Veal Chops

serves 4–6

PREPARATION 2 hrs   COOKING 8 mins

4–6 veal loin chops about

1 in/25mm thick

1½ tablespoons olive oil

1½ tablespoons lemon juice

2 teaspoons lemon pepper

½ cup barbecue relish

(see page 173)

8 oz/250g each potato and

sweet potato, peeled, boiled

and mashed with butter

and milk

1½ teaspoons chopped

fresh chili

PREPARATION

1   Mix the oil, lemon juice and lemon pepper together. Pour into a suitable size non-metallic dish. Add the chops and coat on both sides. Cover and marinate for 2 hours or more in the refrigerator.

2   Prepare sweet potato mash, then stir in the chili. Take all to the barbecue.

AT THE BARBECUE

1   Prepare barbecue for direct-heat cooking. Arrange coals for direct 2 zone heating. Arrange gas burners likewise.

2   Place the chops onto the hot, well-greased grill bars and sear well on both sides. Move to moderate part of the barbecue and continue to cook for about 3 minutes on each side to desired degree. Brush with the seasoning while cooking. Sit the sweet potato mash on barbecue to warm.

3   Top the chops with a good spoonful of relish and garnish with salad greens.

Curried Sirloin Steaks with Mango Relish

serves 4

Curried Sirloin Steaks with Mango Relish

PREPARATION 3 mins   COOKING 15 mins

4 sirloin steaks, ¾ in/2cm thick

1 tablespoon olive oil

1 teaspoon curry powder

¼ teaspoon chili flakes

¼ teaspoon salt

½ cup mango chutney

(see page 175)

2 heads witlof, halved

lengthwise

PREPARATION

1 Wipe the steaks over with damp paper towel. Trim fat if desired. Mix together the olive oil, curry powder, chili flakes and salt in a small bowl. Rub well into the surface of the steaks on both sides. Place chutney in a suitable bowl. Take all to barbecue area.

AT THE BARBECUE

1 Prepare barbecue for direct-heat cooking. Heat coals to medium hot. Preheat gas barbecue to high and turn to medium when steaks go on.

2 Re-brush steaks with oil and curry mixture and place on well-oiled grill bars. Cook for half the desired cooking time (10–12 minutes for medium rare, 13–15 minutes for medium). Brush with oil curry mixture and turn to complete cooking.

3 Grill the witlof for 2–3 minutes each side, brushing with oil and curry mixture as they cook. Serve steaks topped with chutney and the witlof.

Mustard Steak with Garlic Mash

serves 6

Mustard Steak with Garlic Mash

PREPARATION 1 hr 20 mins   COOKING 10–15 mins

1 centre cut slice round steak, about ¾ in/2cm thick and 2 lb/1kg in weight

2 teaspoons olive oil

2 teaspoons garlic, minced

1½ teaspoons mild English mustard

1 lb/500g brown onions

1½ tablespoons olive oil

½ teaspoon salt

3 tablespoons red wine and garlic marinade (see page 189)

PREPARATION

1 Place the steak on a platter, stand to bring to room temperature. Mix the oil, garlic and mustard together. Rub onto both sides of the steak. Stand for 30 minutes before cooking.

2 Prepare the carmelized onion. Peel and halve the onions, slice thinly. Heat oil in a skillet, stir in the onions and cook, stirring for 2 minutes. Turn heat down to low, cover with a lid and leave to sweat for 10 minutes. Increase heat, uncover and stir continuously until brown in color. Stir in salt and marinade, reduce. Prepare garlic mash as on page 83. Take all to barbecue area.

AT THE BARBECUE

1 Prepare barbecue for direct-heat cooking. Heat coals to medium hot and gas barbecue to high, then turn to medium when steaks go on. Place steak on well-oiled grill bars. Cook for 10–12 minutes for medium rare, turning once half way through grilling and 13–15 minutes for medium. Place prepared onion jam and garlic mash at side of grill bars to reheat.

2 Slanting knife at a slight angle, carve the steak in thick slices. Serve on garlic mash and top with a good spoonful of carmelized onion.

Roast Beef with Horseradish Mustard Butter

serves 4–6

Roast Beef with Horseradish Mustard Butter

PREPARATION 6 mins   COOKING 1hr 10 mins

1 boneless sirloin roast,
about 3 lb/1.5kg

ground black pepper

HORSERADISH MUSTARD BUTTER

8 oz/250g butter, softened

2 tablespoons horseradish cream

2 tablespoons Dijon mustard

1 tablespoon finely chopped fresh parsley

10 oz/300g medium-sized chat potatoes, scrubbed and wrapped in foil

PREPARATION

1 Trim off some of the fat from the roast, leaving a thin layer. Season with pepper, set aside.

2 Place softened butter in a bowl and mix lightly with a wooden spoon. Add horseradish cream, mustard and parsley flakes. Mix to combine. Place into a butter crock or suitable dish. Cover and chill until required.

AT THE BARBECUE

1 Prepare the barbecue for indirect cooking. Place a drip pan in the centre. For a charcoal kettle barbecue, heat to medium. For gas kettle or covered gas barbecue heat to hot.

2 Place roast beef on grill directly over drip pan and cook for 1–1½ hours until beef is cooked to your liking. Add foiled wrapped potatoes to barbecue after 1 hour. Place on direct heat each side of meat. Turn each 10–15 minutes. Test with a skewer and remove when done.

3 When roast is cooked transfer to a carving platter. Cover loosely with foil and stand 10 minutes to rest before carving. Serve carved in thick slices, topped with horseradish-mustard butter with potatoes and a side salad.

Honey-Glazed Chops with Pineapple Rice

serves 4

Honey-Glazed Chops with Pineapple Rice

PREPARATION 1hr 25 mins   COOKING 10–15 mins

8 veal short loin chops,
¾ in/15mm thick

MARINADE
salt and pepper
¾ cup honey
½ teaspoon chili powder

PINEAPPLE RICE
1 cup chicken bouillon
½ cup unsweetened
pineapple juice
¾ cup jasmine rice
1 cup peas
½ cup scallions, sliced
3 slices fresh pineapple,
cored and cut into small dice

PREPARATION

1 Season chops with salt and pepper. Coat both sides with honey, then sprinkle with chili powder, cover and refrigerate for 1 hour or more. Retain remaining marinade for glazing.

2 While chops are marinating, prepare the pineapple rice. Place stock and pineapple juice in a skillet, bring to the boil and stir in the rice. Cover and simmer for 15 minutes. Stir in the peas and scallions, cook 3 minutes more. Turn off the heat, stir through the pineapple pieces. Cover and set aside.

AT THE BARBECUE

1 Prepare barbecue for direct-heat cooking. Prepare coals for medium high; the same for gas barbecue, turning heat to medium when cooking begins.

2 Place the chops on the barbecue and cook for 5 minutes, brush with marinade and turn. Cook for a few minutes more, brushing with marinade and turning until chops are cooked and well glazed.

3 Meanwhile, reheat the pineapple rice at the side of the grill plate. Serve chops on a bed of pineapple rice. Drizzle a little fresh marinade over rice if desired.

Plum-Glazed Beef Patties with Noodles

Plum-Glazed Beef Patties with Noodles

PREPARATION 50 mins   **COOKING** 17–20 mins

2 lb/1kg ground beef

1 large onion, finely diced

½ cup dried breadcrumbs

½ teaspoon salt

¼ teaspoon pepper

1 tablespoon sweet plum marinade (see page 187)

2 tablespoons water

BARBECUED NOODLES

1 lb/ 500g Hokkien noodles

1 teaspoon crushed garlic

1 tablespoon finely chopped fresh parsley

1 tablespoon sweet plum marinade (see page 187)

PREPARATION

1 Combine all the ingredients for the patties. Knead by hand to distribute ingredients and make a finer texture. Rest for 20 minutes in refrigerator. With wet hands, shape into 6–8 patties, depending on desired size.

2 Rinse noodles in hot water and separate. Drain very well. Transport all to the barbecue area.

AT THE BARBECUE

1 Prepare barbecue for direct-heat cooking over hot coals. Preheat gas barbecues to hot. Oil the grill bars well.

2 Place a sheet of baking paper over the grill bars and make a few slits in it for airflow. If grilling on the grill plate just place the sheet onto the plate.

3 Place on the patties and cook 6–7 minutes on each side, brushing regularly with marinade to glaze well.

4 Oil the hotplate well or place an oiled oven tray onto the grill bars and heat. Add the noodles, garlic, parsley flakes and plum marinade and toss around. Mix well. Heat through. Serve the patties with noodles and a side salad.

Teriyaki Steak Pockets with Onion Salad

Teriyaki Steak Pockets with Onion Salad

PREPARATION 24 hrs 20 mins   COOKING 17–21 mins

1 thick-cut slice of chuck steak, about ¾ in/2cm thick

¾ cup teriyaki sauce

(see page 186)

ONION SALAD

1 lb/500g medium-sized onions

1 tablespoon salt

½ tablespoon oregano

1 tablespoon finely chopped fresh basil

1 tablespoon finely chopped fresh parsley

2 teaspoons lemon juice

8 pocket breads for serving

2 tomatoes, sliced

PREPARATION

1 Place the steak in a shallow, non-metallic dish and brush well with marinade on both sides. Cover and marinate overnight in the refrigerator. Bring to room temperature before cooking.

2 To prepare the onion salad, peel and finely slice the onions into rings. Place in a bowl, sprinkle with salt and stand for 5 minutes then rub the onion and salt well with the palms of your hands. Rinse well and press out excess water. Place the onions in a bowl, then mix in the oregano, basil, parsley and lemon juice.

AT THE BARBECUE

1 Prepare barbecue for direct-heat cooking. Prepare coals for medium high; do the same for gas barbecue. Turn heat down when meat is placed on it.

2 Oil the grill bars well and place on the chuck steak. Cook for 6–8 minutes on each side, turning once. Brush with marinade during cooking. When cooked to your liking, remove to a platter, cover and rest for 5 minutes. Warm the pocket breads.

3 Slice the meat in ¼ in/5mm-thick slices with knife held at a 45-degree angle. Place the meat on a platter with the onion salad and bread and invite diners to fill their pocket bread. Other salad ingredients may also be offered.

Veal Steak with Red Onions on Toast

Veal Steak with Red Onions on Toast

PREPARATION 45 mins   COOKING 15 mins

4 thin-cut veal leg steaks

1 cup barbecue sauce or

barbecue relish

(see page 173)

4 slices thick bread toast

2 oz/60g butter, softened

2 red onions, thinly sliced

3 tomatoes, thickly sliced

green salad for garnish

PREPARATION

1 Pound the steaks with a meat mallet to an even thickness. Cover and stand for 20 minutes then pour over a little barbecue sauce and stand for 10 minutes more.

2 Prepare remaining ingredients and transtake to the barbecue area.

AT THE BARBECUE

1 Prepare the barbecue using 2 zone method for direct-heat cooking (see page 24). Grease the grill plate well. Place the steaks on hottest part of grill plates. Sear quickly on each side and move to moderate zone of grill plate. Cook for 2 minutes each side.

2 Meanwhile, place the onions on the grill, drizzle with a little oil, toss and cook until golden and soft. Grill the tomatoes. Butter then toast the bread.

3 To assemble, place toast on a warmed plate, place on the steak, drizzle with barbecue sauce or relish. Top with onions and tomato slices. Garnish with green salad.

Beef Satays with Scallions Salad

serves 4

Beef Satays with Scallions Salad

PREPARATION 2 hrs 55 mins   COOKING 7–9 mins

1 skirt steak, about 1½ lb/700g
2 tablespoons vegetable oil
1 tablespoon lime or lemon juice
salt and pepper to taste
½ cup of satay sauce
juice of ½ lemon
1 tablespoon peanut oil
1–2 bunches scallions
20 long satay sticks, soaked for 1 hour

PREPARATION

1 Place the skirt steak on a chopping board. Remove any membrane. With a large knife lightly score the surface in a diagonal criss-cross pattern on both sides. This has a tenderising effect as it cuts through the meat fibres; it also speeds up absorption of marinade.

2 Mix the oil, lime juice, salt and pepper together. Place the steak in a flat, non-metallic dish. Pour in the oil mixture, turn meat to coat both sides. Marinate for 2 hours, turning once. Remove from marinade, pat dry and place on cutting board. Slice the steak across the grain, with knife held at a 45-degree angle to the meat. Strips should be about 5 in/12cm long, ¾ in/2cm wide, ⅛ in/3mm thick.

3 Weave the strips onto soaked satay sticks and gently spread them out flat, not bunched up. Arrange the skewers in a non-metallic flat dish, a lasagna dish for example. Combine lemon juice, satay sauce and peanut oil to form a marinade. Pour over the skewers. Marinate for 30 minutes.

4 Wash the scallions and leave untrimmed. Place in a tray, brush with lemon or lime marinade. Take all to the barbecue.

AT THE BARBECUE

1 Prepare the barbecue for direct-heat cooking, high heat. Oil the grill bars well. Slip a double foil band under the exposed part of the skewers to protect them from burning. Arrange the satays and cook 1–2 minutes per side. Place the scallions onto the grill and grill until soft and browned. Serve immediately.

Veal Rib Roast with Shallots and Garlic

PREPARATION 2 hrs 20 mins   COOKING 1 hr 40 mins

3 lb/1.5kg standing rib roast of veal

¾ cup red wine and garlic marinade (see page 189)

1 lb/500g shallots

2 whole heads of garlic

3 tablespoons vegetable oil mixed with 2 tablespoons water

1½ lb/750g small chat potatoes, washed

SHALLOT DRESSING

1 tablespoon olive oil, combined with 1 teaspoon balsamic vinegar

½ tablespoon fresh oregano

1 tablespoon finely chopped fresh basil

1 tablespoon finely chopped fresh parsley

salt to taste

1 tablespoon cracked black pepper

PREPARATION

1 Place meat into a non-metallic dish. Cover and refrigerate for 2 to 3 hours. Stand at room temperature for 20 minutes before cooking.

2 While veal is standing, trim the root ends of the shallots. Place in a foil baking tray with the garlic heads. Place potatoes in second tray. Toss both with oil water mixture.

AT THE BARBECUE

1 Prepare the barbecue for indirect-heat cooking, medium-high heat, and place a drip tray in the centre. Brush the veal with marinade. Place the shallot and potato trays over indirect heat at each end of the roast. Cover with lid or hood and cook for 40 minutes.

2 Open lid, move trays to direct heat at each side of the roast. Toss the shallots, turn the potatoes. When done, shallots and garlic should be very soft, potatoes tender and browned. Brush roast with marinade close lid and continue to cook 10 minutes.

3 Open lid, brush the roast with marinade. Test the shallots and potatoes and remove if or when ready. Continue to brush the roast with marinade every 8–10 minutes until cooking time of 65 minutes is completed.

4 Remove roast, cover with foil and stand to rest 15 minutes before carving. Slip the shallots and garlic out of their skins, place in serving bowl and toss the shallot dressing gently through. Serve roast surrounded by the roasted vegetables.

serves 14 | Deluxe Hamburgers

PREPARATION 30 mins   COOKING 15–16 mins

BURGER PATTIES

2 lb/1kg ground beef

1 large onion, grated or processed

½ cup dried breadcrumbs

½ teaspoon salt

¼ teaspoon pepper

3 tablespoons tomato ketchup

2 tablespoons water

BUNS AND SUGGESTED FILLINGS

14 hamburger buns

softened butter for spreading

1 lettuce, separated into leaves, washed and drained

1 bunch arugula, washed and drained

2 large onions, thinly sliced and cooked on the hotplate

sandwich cheese slices

1 cup tomato ketchup

1 cup green tomato relish (see page 167)

PREPARATION

1 Combine all the ingredients for the burger patties. Knead by hand to distribute evenly and make the texture finer. Rest for 20 minutes in the refrigerator. With wet hands, shape into 14 flat patties about 3 in/8cm in diameter.

AT THE BARBECUE

1 Place barbecue for direct-heat cooking. Heat until hot. Oil the grill bars, place on the patties and cook for 5–6 minutes on each side. Brush with a little oil as they cook.

2 Split the buns and lightly spread with softened butter. Place buttered side down on hotplate and toast to golden color.

3 To assemble, place a lettuce leaf on bottom half of bun, top with cooked patty, tomato ketchup, onions, cheese slice, arugula leaf and your choice of pickle or relish. Top with remaining bun.

Lamb Fillets with Hot Potato Cakes

serves 4-5

PREPARATION 30 mins   COOKING 18–21 mins

1 ¼ lb/600g lamb fillets

POTATO CAKES

1 ¾ lb/800g potatoes, peeled

1 tablespoon butter

¾ cup sour cream

1 teaspoon chopped chives

⅓ cup all-purpose flour

¾ teaspoon baking powder

½ cup red wine and garlic

marinade (see page 189)

PREPARATION

1 Boil the potatoes until tender, drain and mash. Stir in the butter, sour cream, chives, flour and baking powder. Form into patties using about ⅓ cup of mash for each. Place onto a tray, refrigerate until ready to cook.

AT THE BARBECUE

1 Prepare barbecue for direct-heat cooking. Heat the grill plate to hot and oil well. Place the potato cakes on the grill, cook until brown on both sides. Keep warm.

2 Cook the lamb fillets for 6–8 minutes on the oiled grill plate, turning to cook all sides. Rest 2–3 minutes then diagonally cut into 2cm slices. Heat the sauce. Serve on individual plates on top of potato cakes with the red wine marinade and garnish with arugula.

Moroccan Lamb Cutlets with Couscous

Moroccan Lamb Cutlets with Couscous

PREPARATION 35 mins   COOKING 8–10 mins

12 lamb cutlets, frenched

2 teaspoons olive oil

Moroccan spice mix seasoning

COUSCOUS

1½ cups instant couscous

1½ cups boiling water

½ teaspoon salt

1 tablespoon butter

5 dried apricot halves

2 tablespoons slivered

almonds, toasted

PREPARATION

1   Rub cutlets with a little oil on both sides and sprinkle on both sides with the Moroccan seasoning. Place on a platter, cover and refrigerate for 20 minutes. Stand at room temperature for 15 minutes before cooking.

2   While lamb is standing, place the couscous in a large bowl. Bring water and salt to the boil and pour immediately over the couscous. Stir, then stand covered for 5 minutes or until all water is absorbed.

3   Line the steamer with a circle of baking paper larger than the base. With a skewer punch through the paper to make some holes to enable steam to enter. Spoon the couscous into the steamer. Sprinkle on the apricots, set the steamer over the skillet of boiling water and steam uncovered for 20 minutes. Add the butter and almonds and fork through.

AT THE BARBECUE

1   Prepare the barbecue for 2 zone direct-heat cooking, (see page 24). Place the steamer at the side of hot plate to keep hot.

2   Place the cutlets on hottest part of the grill. Cook for 2 minutes. Move to second zone of grill and cook 2 minutes more. Turn cutlet with tongs, return to hotter grill and cook second side likewise.

3   Tip the steamer with the couscous on its side next to serving platter and pull out the paper, tipping the couscous onto the platter. Mound it high, arrange the cutlets around the couscous and serve immediately.

Doner Kebabs

makes 18–20

Doner Kebabs

PREPARATION 2 hrs   COOKING 2½–3 hrs

FOR THE LAMB

3–4 lb/1½–2kg boneless, lamb forequarter or leg rolled roast

⅓ cup fresh lemon juice

⅓ cup salad oil

2 teaspoons freshly crushed garlic

1 teaspoon fresh oregano leaves

1 tablespoon finely chopped fresh mint

½ teaspoon ground black pepper

1 teaspoon salt or to taste

soaked cotton kitchen string for tying

FILLING

2 tubs prepared hummus dip

1 head lettuce, finely shredded

4 large tomatoes, thinly sliced

2 large onions, thinly sliced

1 tablespoon chili sauce of choice

3 packets large Lebanese flatbread

PREPARATION

1 Untie the roast and open it out. Place skin side down in a flat, non-metallic dish. Mix remaining lamb ingredients together, spoon over surface of lamb to cover and allow to marinate several hours in the refrigerator. When ready to use, reroll and tie with soaked kitchen string.

2 While lamb is marinating, prepare all the filling ingredients and when required transfer to barbecue area.

AT THE BARBECUE

1 Prepare covered barbecue for indirect-heat cooking over medium-high coals, reducing to medium during cooking. Preheat gas barbecues to high. Turn to medium when meat is placed on. Insert a drip tray.

2 Place the lamb roast on greased grill bars over drip tray. Close the lid or hood. Cook for 1¾–2¼ hours, turning the roast after 40 minutes. Roast will be ready when juices run clear when pierced with a skewer or when an inserted meat thermometer reads about 158°F/70°C for medium well done. Remove roast, cover with foil and rest 15 minutes before carving.

3 Carve into thin slices, keep warm. Place the flat breads over the grill bars to heat.

4 Spread the flatbread with hummus, top with lamb slices and salad ingredients and drizzle with chili sauce. Roll up and wrap paper napkin around end.

Honey Garlic Soy Short Loin with Lime

serves 3–4

Honey Garlic Soy Short Loin with Lime

PREPARATION 4 hrs **COOKING** 8 mins

12 thick lamb short loin chops

¾ cup honey

1 teaspoon garlic

2 tablespoons soy sauce

SALSA

5–6 limes

2 medium-sized red onions,
finely diced

1 cup coarsely chopped
arugula leaves

½ teaspoon sugar, or to taste

salt to taste

1 teaspoon chopped
fresh chili

PREPARATION

1 Place the chops in a large, non-metallic dish in one layer. Cover with soy sauce, garlic and honey and marinate for 3–4 hours in refrigerator. Stand at room temperature 20 minutes before cooking.

2 While lamb is marinating, prepare the salsa, peel the limes, removing all pith, cut in half lengthwise. Remove core and seeds and cut into ¼ in/5mm dice.

3 Toss the diced lime, onions, chopped arugula, chili and sugar together. Add salt to taste, place in a bowl and sprinkle with freshly ground black pepper. Refrigerate until serving time. Take all to the barbecue area.

AT THE BARBECUE

1 Prepare the barbecue for 2 zone direct-heat cooking. Oil the grill well. Place meat on hottest part of the grill in rows and cook 4 minutes, brushing with extra marinade twice. Turn the chops, brush with extra marinade, move to second zone to complete cooking until done to your liking. Total cooking time is 6–8 minutes for medium. If marinade is charring, place a sheet of baking paper over the grill and place the chops on the baking paper.

2 Serve with salsa and accompany with barbecued baby sweet corn and other vegetables of choice.

Lemon-lime Butterflied Lamb with Baby Corn

serves 4

Lemon-lime Butterflied Lamb with Baby Corn

PREPARATION 2 hrs 10 mins   COOKING 56–70 mins

3 lb/1½ kg boned leg of lamb

2 teaspoons freshly crushed garlic

1 teaspoon freshly chopped ginger

lemon pepper to sprinkle

1 lb/500g fresh baby corn

1 cup chunky tomato relish (see page 181)

PREPARATION

1 Open out the lamb, place skin-side down on a chopping board. Cut into all the thicker parts of the meat at a 45-degree angle until almost through. Fold back and beat with a meat mallet to flatten to an even thickness, about 1¼ in/3cm thick.

2 Rub the meat surface with the garlic and ginger and sprinkle lightly with lemon pepper. Fold the shank end and the sides into the center to meet, making a flat roast. Pass two long metal skewers through, diagonally, weaving to secure the folded pieces.

3 Cover and refrigerate for several hours or overnight. Stand at room temperature for 20 minutes before cooking. Take the lamb and other ingredients to barbecue area.

AT THE BARBECUE

1 Prepare the barbecue for direct heat. Oil the surface of the meat and place on grill bars, cook each side for 3–5 minutes. Reduce heat to medium or move to a cooler part of the barbecue, cook 20–25 minutes each side, turning once.

2 When cooked, wrap in foil and rest for 10 minutes before carving. While it is resting, put the baby corn on the oiled grill, and toss around to cook. Serve lamb with the baby corn and relish.

Lamb Sirloin with Honey-Glazed Onions

serves 4

Lamb Sirloin with Honey-Glazed Onions

PREPARATION 1 hr 35 mins   COOKING 10–12 mins

2 lamb sirloins, about

12 oz/340g each

sprinkling of salt (optional)

½ cup honey

1 teaspoon freshly minced

garlic

2 tablespoon soy sauce

4 small onions, about 1½ in/

4cm diameter, peeled;

leave root end on

4 slices bread cut ½ in/1cm

thick for croutons

4 oz/115g butter, softened

1 teaspoon horseradish cream

salad mix for serving

PREPARATION

1   Place the lamb sirloins in a flat dish. Coat with soy sauce and sprinkle garlic over evenly. Coat both sides with honey. Cover and refrigerate 1 hour. Remove to room temperature 20 minutes before cooking.

2   Remove crusts from bread. Mix butter and horseradish cream together and spread on both sides of each slice. Cut bread into ½ in/1 cm squares, creating cubes.

3   Quarter the onions. Place a toothpick through centre of thin edge to outer side. Have salad mix prepared.

AT THE BARBECUE

1   Prepare barbecue for 2 zone direct heat grill cooking. Oil the onions and place on cooler zone to cook slowly. Turn often and brush with extra marinade until well cooked and glazed.

2   Place lamb on the hot zone of the grill onto well-oiled grill bars. Cook for 2 minutes to sear, then turn and sear other side. Continue to cook present side for 2–3 minutes more, brushing each 40 seconds with extra marinade. Turn and complete cooking in same fashion. Remove from grill when done to your liking.

3   Toss the bread cubes or croutons on the grill to quickly brown on all sides and to crisp. This can be done simultaneously with cooking the meat.

4   To serve, place the salad on 4 plates, sprinkle over some croutons. Place half a loin on each plate and garnish with glazed onions. Serve immediately.

Mini Lamb Roast with Grilled Asparagus

serves 6

Mini Lamb Roast with Grilled Asparagus

PREPARATION 1 hr 30 mins   COOKING 35–40 mins

2 trim lamb mini roasts,
approximately 1 lb/500g each

½ cup honey

1 teaspoon garlic

2 tablespoons soy sauce

4 small onions, peeled and
quartered

2 bunches fresh asparagus

small bamboo skewers soaked

PREPARATION

1 Place the roasts in a greased foil roasting pan, cover with soy, garlic and honey and leave for 1 or more hours in the refrigerator. Remove 20 minutes before cooking to come to room temperature. Place the onions in the roasting pan around the meat. Brush with marinade.

2 Trim off the woody ends of the asparagus and discard. Place 4 or 5 asparagus side by side on a chopping board, line up the bases evenly. Skewer the asparagus together in 2 places with a small bamboo skewer, just below the tips and 1½ in/ 3cm up from the base. Spread out to make a slight space (⅛ in/3mm) between each asparagus. Place on a tray. Repeat with remainder. Brush both sides with a little oil. Take all to the barbecue area.

AT THE BARBECUE

1 Prepare barbecue for indirect-heat cooking and heat to moderately hot. Place the mini roast tray over indirect heat. Brush meat with marinade, close lid or hood and cook for 15 minutes. Open the cover, turn the roasts and onions and brush them with marinade. Cook a further 10–15 minutes or until cooked to your liking. Remove when cooked, cover and stand 5 minutes.

2 Using tongs, place on the asparagus, and brush tops with marinade. Cook 2–3 minutes. Turn, brush again and cook until crisp tender. Remove to plate.

3 Carve the roast and serve with the onions and asparagus. Pour any juices from the pan over the lamb.

Macadamia-Crusted Lamb Racks

serves 4–5

Macadamia-Crusted Lamb Racks

PREPARATION 2 hrs 12 mins   COOKING 1 hr

3 lamb racks (3–4 cutlets each)

2 teaspoons oil

2 cups soft white breadcrumbs

2 tablespoons melted butter

½ cup chopped macadamia nuts

1 teaspoon fresh oregano

1 tablespoon finely chopped fresh basil

1 tablespoon finely chopped fresh parsley

½ teaspoon lemon pepper

1 beaten egg to bind

2 slender sweet potatoes

3 small onions, peeled and quartered with root end attached

PREPARATION

1 Trim some of the fat from the racks, leaving only a thin layer.

2 Place breadcrumbs into a bowl. Add butter, macadamia nuts, oregano, basil, parsley and lemon pepper. Mix to distribute ingredients evenly, then add only enough egg to just bind the mixture (not too moist). Press firmly onto each rack. Place in a tray, cover carefully with wrap, refrigerate.

3 Peel the sweet potato and cut diagonally into ¾ in/2cm slices. Place lamb with the onions in a foil roasting pan and drizzle with a little oil.

AT THE BARBECUE

1 Prepare covered barbecue for indirect cooking. Heat coals to medium high, gas barbecue to high. Reduce heat to medium when food is placed. Place the foil tray with the sweet potato and onions on indirect heat, cover with lid or hood and cook for 15 minutes.

2 Open lid, move the potato tray to direct heat and turn the vegetables. Place the lamb racks in the foil tray over indirect heat or place directly onto the grill bars over a drip tray. Cover with hood and cook for 35 minutes.

3 Remove lamb when done and rest 10 minutes before serving. Remove vegetables. Serve the lamb racks on heated plates with a serving of vegetables.

Chump Chops with Garlic Mash

serves 4

Chump Chops with Garlic Mash

PREPARATION 2 hrs 10 mins   COOKING 20 mins

6–8 lamb chump chops

1 cup red wine and garlic marinade (see page 189)

GARLIC MASH

2 lb/1kg potatoes, peeled and cut

4 teaspoons freshly crushed garlic

½ cup milk

3 tablespoons butter

salt and pepper to taste

½ cup carmelized onion and red wine reduction (see page 176)

PREPARATION

1 Trim the side fat from the chops leaving a thin strip. Coat both sides with the marinade. Cover and marinate for 2 hours in the refrigerator. Bring to room temperature before cooking.

2 Cook the potatoes until soft in boiling salted water. Drain well and mash in the skillet while hot. Add the garlic, butter and milk. Take all to the barbecue area.

AT THE BARBECUE

1 Prepare barbecue for direct-heat cooking. Heat medium high for charcoal, high for gas, then turn to medium high.

2 Oil the grill bars well and place the chops on top. Cook for 6–8 minutes on each side or until done to your liking. Brush with extra marinade at intervals. Reheat the potato at side of barbecue. Pour the wine and onion reduction into a small pan, then place it on the barbecue to heat.

3 To serve, place a serve of potato on each plate, lightly drizzle the surface of the potato with half of the heated red wine reduction and place on the chops on top. Pour remaining sauce down centre of chops. Serve with vegetables of choice and garnish with finely shredded flat-leaf parsley.

Lamb Kebabs with Pita Bread

PREPARATION 2 hrs 15 mins   **COOKING** 10–14 mins

1½ lb/750g boneless lamb, cut into ¾ in/2cm cubes

½ cup lemon juice

2 teaspoons fresh oregano

1 tablespoon finely chopped fresh parsley

2 bay leaves, crumbled

1 small onion, chopped

¼ cup olive oil

ground black pepper

8 bamboo skewers, soaked

FOR SERVING

2 packets pocket pita breads

2 tubs tabouli

1 bottle chili and garlic sauce

PREPARATION

1 Place lamb cubes in a bowl with remaining ingredients except skewers. Mix to coat the lamb well. Cover and marinate in refrigerator for 2 hours or more. Thread 5–6 pieces of lamb onto each skewer. Retain the marinade. Place kebabs on a tray. Take to barbecue area with breads, tabouli and remaining marinade.

AT THE BARBECUE

1 Prepare barbecue grill or hotplate for direct-heat cooking. Heat to high and oil well. Place on the kebabs. Cook and turn when needed. Baste frequently with remaining marinade. Cook for 4–6 minutes each side. Do not overcook. Meat should feel springy when pressed. Place the pocket pita breads at side of barbecue plate to warm up.

2 To serve, open pocket and spoon in a good serving of tabouli, add kebab skewer and a squeeze of sauce. Pass to guest and remind them to pull out the skewer before eating.

serves 4–6

Warm Lamb Greek Salad

PREPARATION 2 hrs   COOKING 20 mins

6 lambs fillets

2 tablespoons olive oil

1½ tablespoons fresh oregano

8 oz/250g Greek feta cheese

8 oz/250g truss cherry
tomatoes

1 continental cucumber

1 medium-sized red onion,
peeled and halved

16 Kalamata olives

5 oz/150g mixed salad greens

PREPARATION

1 Remove sinew from the lamb fillets with a sharp knife. Pour the olive oil over the lamb and sprinkle with the dried oregano. Rub well into the meat.

2 Place in the refrigerator and marinate for a few hours. While meat is marinating, cut the feta into ½ in/1cm cubes. Slice the cucumber into thin slices. Slice the red onion thinly. Place in a salad bowl with the olives and mixed salad greens. Toss.

AT THE BARBECUE

1 Prepare the barbecue for direct-heat cooking. Heat to high and oil the grill bars well. Remove stems from tomatoes and place onto grill. Cook until they begin to collapse. Add to the salad bowl. Toss.

2 Place lamb fillets on hot grill, cook for 5 minutes each side. Cover and rest for 5 minutes, then slice each on the diagonal into 4 pieces. Arrange the salad and place sliced lamb on top with a little oil and vinegar dressing.

Pork Fillet with Arugula, Apple and Parmesan Salad

serves 4

PREPARATION 2 hrs 15 mins   COOKING 25 mins

1 lb/500g pork fillet

1 cup red wine and garlic
marinade (see page 189)

SALAD

7 oz/200g wild arugula

2 apples

shaved Parmesan

½ cup Italian dressing

PREPARATION

1 Trim the pork fillet of any sinew and fat and place in a shallow non-metallic dish. Pour over enough marinade to coat both sides. Cover and refrigerate for several hours or overnight.

2 Quarter the apple and slice thinly. Oil the grill bars and place on the apple slices. Cook until there are dark char lines and the apple is soft. Set aside. Wash the arugula and drain well.

AT THE BARBECUE

1 Prepare the barbecue for direct heating. Oil the grill bars and place on the marinated pork fillet. Cook for 10 minutes each side, brushing with the extra marinade. Remove the pork and rest in a warm place while preparing the salad.

2 In a large bowl place the arugula, grilled apples and a good handful of shaved Parmesan.

3 Slice the pork fillet on the diagonal ½ in/1cm thick and add to the salad.

4 Divide up the salad onto 4 dinner plates and dress each salad with Italian dressing.

Rolled Loin of Pork with Apricot Stuffing

serves 6–8

Rolled Loin of Pork with Apricot Stuffing

PREPARATION 35 mins   COOKING 1 hr 10 mins

4 lb/2kg boned loin of pork
with flap on and rind removed

salt and pepper to taste

¾ cup apricot marinade
(see page 169)

STUFFING

2 cups soft breadcrumbs

1 tablespoon finely chopped
fresh sage

½ teaspoon onion flakes

⅓ cup finely chopped dried
apricots

1 tablespoon apricot
marinade (see page 169)

PREPARATION

1   With a small pointed knife, score the outside fat layer in a diamond pattern. Turn over, fat side down, and sprinkle the meat lightly with salt and pepper.

2   Mix the stuffing ingredients together and place under the flap, packing it up against the loin meat. Leave 1 in/25mm before the edge of the flap. Press down the flap tightly and fasten with skewers. Tie the roast with kitchen string at 1 in/25mm intervals. Remove skewers. Brush over with marinade.

3   Refrigerate until ready to use. Then stand at room temperature for 20 minutes before cooking.

AT THE BARBECUE

1   Prepare barbecue for indirect-heat cooking medium heat and set in a drip pan. Place the roast over the drip pan, cover with lid or hood and cook for 50 minutes.

2   Commence glazing with the marinade every 10 minutes for 45–50 minutes or until internal temperature on a meat thermometer reaches about 190°F/76°C. When inserting the meat thermometer, take care to insert it into the centre of the loin meat and not into the flap and stuffing.

3   When cooked, remove from heat, wrap in foil and rest 15 minutes before carving. Place the apple rings over indirect heat. Brush with marinade, close cover and cook for about 8–10 minutes. Turn and glaze other side. Serve with barbecued vegetables (see page 157).

Pork Spare Ribs on Sourdough

serves 8–10

Pork Spare Ribs on Sourdough

PREPARATION 35 mins   COOKING 28 mins

3 lb/1.5 kg pork spare ribs

1 cup barbecue sauce

1 round loaf sourdough bread

1 cup mango chutney

(see page 175)

GARLIC BUTTER

6 oz/170g salted butter at

room temperature

4 teaspoons freshly crushed

garlic

½ teaspoon lemon pepper

PREPARATION

1 Sprinkle each spare rib lightly on both sides with meat tenderiser. Stand at room temperature for 20 minutes.

2 Cut sourdough bread into ¾ in/15mm thick slices. Halve the larger centre slices. Mix garlic butter ingredients together and spread on both sides of the bread. Take a small bowl, a brush, barbecue sauce and chutney to barbecue area.

AT THE BARBECUE

1 Prepare barbecue for direct-heat cooking on high. Oil the grill bars or plate well. Brush the ribs lightly on both sides with the barbecue sauce and place on the hottest part of the grill. Sear for 2–3 minutes on each side.

2 Brush top of ribs with the sauce and turn sauce side down onto the grill. Cook for 8 minutes then brush the top side with sauce and turn. Cook for 8 minutes more. Brush once more and turn and cook for 2 minutes. Repeat and cook until done to your liking.

3 During last stage of cooking place the garlic bread onto the grill. Cook to toast both sides. To serve, place a rib onto each bread slice and top with chutney. Serve immediately.

Smokey Barbecue Spare Ribs

Smokey Barbecue Spare Ribs

PREPARATION 2 hrs 10 mins   COOKING 30–35 mins

2 x 2 lb/1kg racks American-style ribs

¾ cup barbeque relish (see page 173)

¼ cup olive oil

PREPARATION

1 Place the ribs in a large, non-metallic dish. Thoroughly combine relish and the oil and liberally brush relish onto ribs. Cover and marinate in refrigerator for several hours or overnight, turning occasionally.

2 Take 2 large sheets of heavy-duty foil and place on a work surface. Place a rack of ribs on each. Generously cover both sides of ribs with extra marinade. Wrap into a double-folded parcel, making sure all joins are well sealed to prevent leakage. Carefully place parcel onto a tray, taking care not to tear the foil. Refrigerate if not cooking immediately.

AT THE BARBECUE

1 Prepare the barbecue for direct-heat cooking. Place a wire cake rack on the grill bars to stand 1 in/25mm above grill. Place the foil parcels on the rack and cook for 10 minutes on each side for a total of 20 minutes.

2 Remove to a plate. Open foil and discard. Lift ribs onto the rack. Continue cooking and brush with extra relish, turning until ribs are well browned and crisp, for about 10 minutes. Cut between the ribs, pile onto a platter and serve immediately.

Pork Loin Caesar

serves 4

Pork Loin Caesar

PREPARATION 10 mins   COOKING 15–20 mins

4 pork loin steaks,
6–7 oz/170–200g each

1 tablespoon celery salt

1 tablespoon pepper

1 tablespoon onion powder

1 tablespoon sweet paprika

1 loaf white bread

4 tablespoons olive oil

½ tablespoon fresh oregano

1 tablespoon finely chopped
fresh basil

2 tablespoons finely chopped
fresh parsley

4 baby Romain lettuce hearts

2 anchovies, chopped

whole egg mayonnaise

shaved Parmesan cheese

PREPARATION

1 Combine salt, pepper, onion powder and paprika and sprinkle liberally over loin steaks. To prepare the croutons, remove the crust from the bread. Cut bread into ¾ in/2cm thick slices and cut into cubes.

2 Mix the oil, oregano, basil and parsley together and lightly coat the bread. Place on a very hot grill or plate and toast until brown and crisp. Pull the lettuce hearts apart, wash well, trim off the ends and shake dry.

AT THE BARBECUE

1 Prepare the barbecue for direct-heat cooking. Oil the grill well. Cook the steaks on the grill for 6–7 minutes each side. Place loins on the bread and serve on dinner plates. Top them with the lettuce, Parmesan and anchovies. Drizzle some mayonnaise over.

Crusted Pork Fillets with Honey Mustard Sauce

Crusted Pork Fillets with Honey Mustard Sauce

PREPARATION 10 mins   COOKING 35–40 mins

2 pork fillets, about 1 lb/450g each

CRUST TOPPING

2 cups fresh white breadcrumbs

2 oz/60g butter, melted

1 teaspoon freshly crushed garlic

½ tablespoon fresh oregano

1 tablespoon finely chopped fresh basil

1 tablespoon finely chopped fresh parsley

salt and pepper to taste

1½ tablespoons pine nuts, toasted (optional)

1 egg

HONEY MUSTARD SAUCE

juice of 1 lemon

2 tablespoons wholegrain mustard

1 teaspoon cornstarch

1 tablespoon honey

TO SERVE

2–3 pears, quartered, cored

1 tablespoon butter, melted

PREPARATION

1 Remove any silver skin from fillets, easing them off with a small sharp knife. Trim off tapering ends from the fillets, (reserve for other use). Cut each fillet across into 3 even pieces about 2¾ in/7cm, depending on length of fillet. Place fillets in a well-greased shallow baking tray.

2 Combine all the crust topping ingredients except the egg. Beat the egg well and add just enough to moisten the crumbs. Divide the mixture and press a portion evenly onto the surface of each fillet portion.

AT THE BARBECUE

1 Prepare barbecue for indirect-heat cooking. (For charcoal heat to medium high; gas heat to high and turn to medium when food goes on.)

2 Place the tray with the fillets over indirect heat and cook with lid or hood down for 25–30 minutes or until done to your liking.

3 Remove tray, cover and rest meat for 5 minutes. Meanwhile, place the pears and lemons on direct heat and cook for 2 minutes each side, brushing with melted butter. Continue cooking until crisp tender and nicely colored. Combine sauce ingredients and heat on a medium heat for 4 minutes.

4 To serve, swirl some sauce onto platter and place the crusted fillets on top. Garnish with the grilled pears and lemons.

serves 4

Teriyaki Pork Steaks

PREPARATION 2 hrs   COOKING 15–20 mins

4 butterflied pork loin steaks

1 cup Teriyaki sauce

(see page 186)

3½ oz/100g snow peas,

strings removed

1 red pepper

1 yellow pepper

1 small bunch scallions

watercress for garnish

PREPARATION

1 Place the steaks into a shallow dish and pour over half cup of the marinade to cover the steaks well. Cover and place into refrigerator for a few hours or overnight. Cut the peppers into ¾ in/2cm pieces. Slice the scallions into 1¼ in/3cm lengths.

AT THE BARBECUE

1 Prepare the barbecue for direct-heat cooking. Oil the grill well. Heat until hot. Place the pork steaks on the grill. Cook for 5–7 minutes on each side, brushing with extra marinade while they are cooking.

2 Brush all the vegetables with some of the marinade and cook on the grill until they are colored and tender. Place each steak onto a dinner plate and top with the cooked vegetables. Garnish with the watercress.

Marinated Pork T-bone Steak

serves 4

Marinated Pork T-bone Steak

PREPARATION 4 hrs 10 mins   COOKING 20 mins

4–6 thick pork loin chops

⅓ cup olive oil

¼ cup soy sauce

1 teaspoon freshly chopped ginger

2 teaspoons French mustard

¼ teaspoon cracked black pepper

wholegrain mustard

mayonaise

TO GARNISH

2 oranges, unpeeled, thinly sliced

watercress sprigs

PREPARATION

1 In a small bowl, mix the oil, soy sauce, ginger, mustard and pepper together. Rub the mixture well into both sides of the chops, and then place in a shallow dish. Cover and marinate 4 hours or more in the refrigerator. Reserve remaining marinade. Prepare garnish. Take all to the barbecue area.

AT THE BARBECUE

1 Prepare barbecue for direct-heat cooking to high heat. Oil the grill bars well. Place on the chops. Cook for 7–8 minutes each side or until cooked through. Turn the chops once and brush occasionally with marinade.

2 Grill the orange slices 1 minute on each side, brushing lightly with marinade. Remove chops to a warmed platter and spoon a little sauce along centre of chops. Top with a drizzle of mayonaise. Garnish with the orange and watercress. Serve remaining sauce in a sauce jug.

Chili Honey Pork Roast

serves 6–8

Chili Honey Pork Roast

PREPARATION 20 mins   COOKING 2 hrs 25 mins

4–5 lb/2–2.5kg boneless pork leg or easy carve leg roast

½ teaspoon salt

¾ cup honey

1 tablespoon freshly chopped chili

zest of 1 lemon

2 lb/1kg potatoes, peeled and cut into wedges

1½ teaspoons lemon pepper

1 teaspoon freshly crushed garlic

¼ cup oil

⅓ cup water

1 head radicchio lettuce

PREPARATION

1 To make glaze, combine honey, chili and lemon zest. Brush the surface of the meat generously with glaze. Refrigerate, covered, until ready to use. Stand at room temperature 20 minutes before cooking.

2 Place potato wedges in a foil tray. Mix lemon pepper, garlic, oil and water together. Pour over potatoes.

3 Cut the radicchio in half lengthwise. Cut each half into 3 wedges. Insert a small bamboo skewer from centre of outside edge to centre of thin wedge edge to keep the wedges from falling apart.

AT THE BARBECUE

1 Prepare covered barbecue for indirect-heat cooking, charcoal to medium high and gas to high turned down to medium when food is placed in.

2 Place the roast on the well-oiled bars over the drip tray. Place the potatoes next to the roast over indirect heat. Brush roast with glaze, close cover and cook for 60 minutes.

3 Move the tray of potatoes over direct heat and turn the potatoes. Brush the roast again with glaze, close hood and continue to cook for 1 hour, brushing the roast with glaze every 15 minutes.

4 When potatoes are browned, remove and keep hot. Roast is cooked when juices run clear when pricked with a skewer, or internal temperature on a meat thermometer is about 155°F/68°C for medium–well done. Remove roast to a platter. Rest for 15 minutes.

5 Reheat the potatoes. Brush both sides of the radicchio wedges with the marinade and grill over direct heat for 3–5 minutes, brushing with glaze. Serve with roast and potatoes.

Teriyaki Pork Skewers

serves 6–8

Teriyaki Pork Skewers

PREPARATION 12 hrs   COOKING 12–15 mins

3 lb/1½ kg boneless shoulder of pork

1 cup Teriyaki sauce (see page 186)

12 oz/350g potatoes, peeled and cut

12 oz/350g sweet potatoes, peeled and cut

1 teaspoon freshly chopped chili

1 tablespoon butter

1½ cups Greek-style yogurt

8–10 bamboo skewers, soaked in water for 30 minutes

PREPARATION

1 Cut the pork into 1 in/25mm cubes. Place cubes in a bowl and pour over marinade to coat well, but keep a little to brush with while cooking. Cover and marinate in refrigerator for 12 hours or overnight to tenderise.

2 Cook all potatoes in boiling salted water. Drain well and mash. Add the chili and butter and mix. Add half of the red wine and garlic marinade. Add extra if needed to make a fluffy mash.

AT THE BARBECUE

1 Prepare barbecue for direct-heat cooking and heat to hot. Turn gas barbecue down to medium hot when food is placed on. Set the skillet of mash at the cooler side to reheat. Put remaining red wine and garlic marinade in a small skillet and heat.

2 Place the pork skewers on the grill. Cook, turning and brushing with extra marinade, for 12–15 minutes or until cooked to your liking.

3 To serve, pile mash in centre of individual plates and top with skewers. Drizzle yogurt over mash and season librally with cracked pepper. Serve with salad accompaniment.

Honey Citrus Thick Loin Chops

serves 4-6

PREPARATION 30 mins   COOKING 30 mins

6 thick-cut pork loin chops

MARINADE

2 tablespoons honey

1 tablespoon orange zest

¼ cup orange juice

1½ tablespoons soy sauce

1½ tablespoons Dijon mustard

2 teaspoons freshly crushed garlic

1 teaspoon freshly chopped ginger

POTATOES AND GARNISH

3 lb/1.5kg medium-sized Kipfler potatoes

2 tablespoons butter

1 teaspoon crushed garlic

1 lemon, halved

PREPARATION

1 Wipe over the chops with clean kitchen towel, trim off fat. Mix the marinade ingredients Brush half of the marinade onto both sides of the chops. Stand for 20 minutes at room temperature, or longer in the refrigerator, before cooking. Scrub the potatoes and wrap each in foil, while marinating chops.

AT THE BARBECUE

1 Prepare barbecue for indirect-heat cooking, Insert a drip tray. Heat charcoal to medium high; gas to high and turn to medium when food is placed on.

2 Place the chops on the well-oiled grill bars over the drip tray. Place the potatoes in a foil tray and stand over direct heat. Close lid and cook for 7 minutes.

3 Open hood. Test and turn the potatoes and brush the chops with marinade. Cook for 7 minutes more.

4 Remove potatoes, brush chops with marinade and turn. Close hood, cook chops for 5 minutes. Test to determine further cooking time. Brush regularly with marinade and cook until done to your liking. Remove chops, cover and rest for 5 minutes.

5 Place the lemon halves over direct heat, brush with marinade. Cook for 2 minutes each side while brushing with marinade until golden and skin is soft.

6 Unwrap potatoes and cut in half. Brush with garlic butter. Serve the chops with the grilled Kipfler potatoes and lemon.

Quick Chicken Focaccia with Sweet Chili Sauce

serves 4

PREPARATION 6 mins   COOKING 10–15 mins

1 lb/500g chicken tenderloins

1 tablespoon mixed herbs

1 large eggplant, cut into

6 slices

2 red peppers, cut down

the 4 sides

7 oz/200g cup mushrooms,

wiped over with damp paper

6 individual focaccia breads

3 oz/90g butter, softened

1 teaspoon freshly crushed

garlic

sweet chili sauce to taste

8 oz/250g mixed lettuce

PREPARATION

1 Sprinkle the chicken tenderloins with the mixed herbs. Prepare the vegetables.

2 Mix the butter with the garlic. Split the focaccia bread and lightly spread with the garlic butter. Take chicken, vegetables and bread to the barbecue area.

AT THE BARBECUE

1 Prepare the barbecue for direct-heat cooking. Heat to medium high. Arrange all ingredients on well-oiled grill plate, leaving focaccia until last. Cook chicken tenderloins and vegetables on each side until ready. Bell pepper will take longer. As they are cooked remove to a tray. Place bread buttered side down and lightly toast.

2 To assemble, place greens and eggplant on base. Top with chicken, cover with mushrooms, then bell pepper. Drizzle each layer lightly with chili sauce. Cover with top and serve immediately.

Barbecued Drumsticks with Asian Flavor

Barbecued Drumsticks with Asian Flavor

PREPARATION 12 hrs 45 mins   **COOKING** 1 hr 40 mins

4 lb/2kg chicken drumsticks, medium size

½ cup fresh lemon juice

1 tablespoon salad oil

1 teaspoon herb salt

½ cup honey

3 tablespoons soy sauce

1 teaspoon freshly chopped garlic

1 teaspoon freshly chopped ginger

4 oz/125g fresh baby corn

4 scallions (not too thin), trimmed and sliced on sharp diagonal

PREPARATION

1   Place drumstick in a large non-metallic container, preferably in one layer. Mix lemon juice, oil, ginger, garlic, herb salt, honey and soy together. Pour over the drumsticks, reserving a small quantity to coat the vegetables. Coat both sides of the drumstick, cover and marinate in the refrigerator for several hours or overnight. Turn in the marinade at least once if you have a double layer, move the top layer to the bottom. Stand at room temperature 20 minutes before cooking.

2   Prepare scallions, and baby corn. Take chicken and vegetables to barbecue area.

AT THE BARBECUE

1   Prepare barbecue for indirect-heat cooking. Place a drip pan containing 1 cup of water in place. Place the drumsticks directly onto the well-oiled grill bars over the drip pan. Cook for 30 minutes with lid on, and then for 30 minutes with lid off. Brush drumsticks with the extra marinade and turn.

2   Close lid, cook 8–10 minutes, turn and brush with marinade and repeat every 10 minutes for a total of 40 minutes or until cooked through to the bone.

3   In the last 10 minutes of cooking, place a sheet of foil on grill bars over direct heat. Place on the baby corn. Brush with marinade and cook 5 minutes. Turn, brush with marinade. Place on the scallion slices, splash with a little marinade and toss. Serve hot.

Peanut-Crusted Chicken Satays

makes 18 skewers

Peanut-Crusted Chicken Satays

PREPARATION 2 hrs 10 mins   COOKING 5 mins

3 chicken breast fillets, boned, approximately 10 oz/300g each

1 cup peanut butter

½ cup honey

2 tablespoons sweet chili sauce

¾ cup unsalted roasted peanuts, crushed

20 bamboo skewers, soaked in water for 15 minutes

1 continental cucumber pared into ribbons with a vegetable peeler, for garnish

PREPARATION

1 Place chicken fillets, smooth side down between 2 pieces of plastic wrap. Pound with a meat mallet to even out the thickness. Cut into 1 in/25mm wide strips. Place into a flat, non-metallic container.

2 Combine peanut butter, honey and sweet chili sauce into a marinade and thin with a little water if necessary. Pour in about ½ cup of marinade, turn to coat both sides and marinate for 2 hours or more in the refrigerator.

3 Weave 1 long strip or 2 short strips onto each skewer, but do not bunch up. Brush both sides with marinade and discard the remainder. Refrigerate until ready to cook. Take 1 cup fresh marinade from the bottle, place in a bowl to use for brushing during cooking. Take to the barbecue

AT THE BARBECUE

1 Prepare the barbecue for direct-heat cooking. Place the skewers on well-oiled grill bars or grill plate. Cook 2 minutes on each side, brushing often with the marinade.

2 Place a piece of foil on a flat tray and sprinkle over the crushed peanuts. As satays come off the grill, press each side onto the peanuts and place on a warmed platter. Garnish with cucumber ribbons. If desired, mix ¾ cup fresh marinade with 2 tablespoons lemon or lime juice and use as extra sauce.

serves 4

Tasty Chicken Wings

PREPARATION 4 hrs 5 mins   **COOKING** 55 mins

4 lb/2kg chicken wings

1¼ cups honey

juice of 1 orange

1 tablespoon finely chopped fresh parsley

1 tablespoon finely chopped fresh oregano

1 teaspoon allspice

2 teaspoons soy sauce

2 limes, sliced into thin circles

2 scallions, diagonally sliced

PREPARATION

1 Place wings in a large stainless steel baking dish. Combine honey, orange juice, herbs, soy sauce and allspice to form marinade and pour over the wings. Coat both sides. Cover and marinate in refrigerator for at least 4 hours or, preferably, overnight.Prepare limes and scallions and take with chicken to the barbecue area.

AT THE BARBECUE

1 Prepare barbecue for indirect-heat cooking and heat to medium. Add half cup of water to the wings in the dish. Turn and mix through, then spread wings to a single layer. Cover with a lid, and place over indirect heat for 45–50 minutes. Turn wings occasionally.

2 Lift the wings with tongs and place on well-oiled grill bars over direct heat for 1–2 minutes each side to crisp.

3 Place lime slices on grill for 1 minute each side, brushing with a little marinade. Remove chicken wings to a platter, garnish with lime slices and sprinkle with scallions.

Cajun Chicken

serves 4

Cajun Chicken

PREPARATION 2 hrs 40 mins   COOKING 47 mins

4 chicken breasts on the bone, skin in

1 tablespoon olive oil

2 tablespoons Cajun spice

1 tablespoon barbecue sauce

2 eggplant, cut into ¾ in/15mm-thick round slices

½ cup tomato and chili pickle (see page 185)

2 sprigs fresh oregano

PREPARATION

1 Rinse the chicken, pat well to dry If necessary, smooth the skin over the breast.

2 Rub the chicken all over with oil, then rub the Cajun spices over with fingers, massaging in. Place in deep container, skin side up. Cover with lid or wrap that does not touch the top of the chicken. Refrigerate for 2 hours or more or just stand at room temperature for 20 minutes, then cook. Longer marinating time increases flavor.

3 Cut eggplant slices just before cooking. Have oil and brush ready. Take all to the barbecue area, including barbecue sauce and pickle.

AT THE BARBECUE

1 Prepare barbecue for indirect-heat cooking; Insert a drip tray. Heat to medium.

2 Place the chicken breasts, skin side up, onto the oiled grill over the drip tray. Close the lid or hood and cook for 40 minutes; no need to turn. During the final cooking, open lid and brush lightly with barbecue sauce a few times to give a glaze. Chicken is cooked when juices run clear when pricked with a skewer. Remove from grill and keep hot.

3 Before the final cooking, place a shallow oven tray over the direct heat section. When it is hot, brush with oil. Brush the eggplant on both sides with oil and place on the hot tray, turn and cook other side after 2 minutes. Remove when done. Serve the chicken on a bed of eggplant. Place a tablespoon of pickle on top of each chicken breast and garnish with a sprig of fresh oregano.

Barbecued Turkey Roll

serves 4

Barbecued Turkey Roll

PREPARATION 10 mins   COOKING 1–1¼ hrs

1 turkey breast, skin on
(approximately 2 lb/1kg)
chicken seasoning
⅔ cup red wine and garlic
marinade (see page 189)

STUFFING

2 cups fresh bread crumbs
1 medium red onion, finely
chopped
2 tablespoons toasted pine
nuts
1½ tablespoons golden raisins,
chopped lightly
1 tablespoon melted butter
1 tablespoon red wine
and garlic marinade
(see page 189)
1 tablespoon finely chopped
fresh parsley

PREPARATION

1 Place turkey breast, skin-side down, on chopping board. Make a cut almost through into the thick part of breast, slanting knife at a 45-degree angle. Open out and pound the area with the side of meat mallet to thin out evenly. Sprinkle with the chicken seasoning.

2 Mix stuffing ingredients together and place along the centre of the length. Form into a roll and secure with skewers. Tie with kitchen string at 1 in/25mm intervals, then remove the skewers. Brush all over with the marinade. Take all to the barbecue.

AT THE BARBECUE

1 Prepare barbecue for indirect-heat cooking, medium-high heat. Place in a drip tray.

2 Place the turkey roll onto well-oiled grill bars over the drip tray. Cover with lid or hood and cook for 1–1¼ hours brushing frequently with marinade. Turkey is done when juices run clear when pierced with a skewer.

3 When turkey roll is cooked, remove and stand, covered, in foil for 10 minutes before carving. Serve with roasted vegetables or green salad.

serves 4

Tandoori Chicken Pieces

PREPARATION 6 hrs 10 mins   COOKING 40 mins

6 chicken Maryland pieces,
skin off

salt

7 oz/200mL natural yogurt

tandoori paste to taste

1 tablespoon butter or ghee,
melted

TO SERVE

crisp lettuce leaves

1 lemon

1 packet flatbread

(Lebanese bread)

PREPARATION

1 Prick the meat all over with a skewer. Sprinkle lightly with salt.

2 Mix the yogurt with 4 tablespoons of the tandoori paste, adding more to taste if desired. With fingers, rub mixture all over the chicken pieces, rubbing well into the slashes. Place into a non-metallic dish, cover and marinate in refrigerator for 6 hours or overnight.

3 Place chicken on a greased baking tray. Pour the excess marinade from the dish into a bowl. Stir butter or ghee into the marinade. Transfer all to the barbecue area.

AT THE BARBECUE

1 Prepare the barbecue for indirect-heat cooking. Set up a drip pan with a cup of water in the pan.

2 Place the chicken on the well-oiled grill bars over the drip pan. Cover and cook for 40 minutes or until cooked. Brush with the reserved marinade at 10 minute intervals for first half of cooking, then at 5 minute intervals. At the last 5 minutes, place flatbreads into barbecue to heat over direct heat.

3 Remove from grill. Place on a platter lined with lettuce leaves. Garnish with lemon slices. Cut each flatbread into 6 triangular pieces and serve with the tandoori chicken.

Spiced Chicken Breast

Spiced Chicken Breast

PREPARATION 2 hrs   COOKING 20 mins

4 chicken breasts, boned and skin off

2 tablespoons oil

2 tablespoons Cajun spice mix

3–4 medium zucchini

4 serves of Cajun Chat potatoes (see page 166)

PREPARATION

1 In a shallow dish, place the chicken breasts. Pour over the oil, and then sprinkle the breasts with the Cajun spice mix. Rub well into the chicken, and place in the refrigerator for several hours or overnight.

2 While chicken is marinating, wash zucchini under cold running water, and cut off the ends. Slice on the diagonal to ¾ in/15mm thick, sprinkle with a little oil and some extra Cajun spice mix.Remove the chicken from the refrigerator.

AT THE BARBECUE

1 Prepare the barbecue for direct-heat cooking. Place the chicken breasts on well-oiled grill bars in a neat row and cook for 10 minutes on each side. During the last 5–8 minutes, grill the zucchini. Place on the grill and cook for 3–4 minutes each side. Brush with more oil during cooking.

2 To serve, slice the chicken breasts on the diagonal into 4 slices, Place on top of the Cajun chat potatoes with the grilled zucchini.

Jasmine Chicken

serves 4–6

Jasmine Chicken

PREPARATION 2 hrs   COOKING 10–12 mins

6 chicken thigh fillets

salt and pepper to taste

¾ cup Thai marinade

(see page 183)

8 oz/250g snow peas, strings
removed and rinsed

1 red pepper, julienned

TO SERVE

2 cups of jasmine rice,
steamed

watercress for garnish

PREPARATION

1 With side of a meat mallet, pound out the thigh fillets slightly to an even thickness. Cut each fillet into 2 pieces and place in a non-metallic dish in a single layer. Pour over enough marinade to cover completely. Cover with cling wrap and marinate in refrigerator for several hours or overnight.

2 While chicken is marinating, wrap the snow peas in 2 pieces of foil making a parcel fold. Steam the rice.

3 Remove the chicken fillets from the marinade and place on plate. Discard the marinade. Take remainder of fresh marinade and all other ingredients to the barbecue area.

AT THE BARBECUE

1 Prepare barbecue for direct-heat cooking and heat to hot. Arrange chicken on well-oiled grill bars. Place snow pea pack to the side. Cook chicken for 3–4 minutes each side, brushing frequently with fresh marinade until glazed and golden. Cook snow peas parcel on one side for 2 minutes, then turn parcel over and cook for another 2 minutes.

2 To serve, mix the chicken, snow peas and pepper through the rice and garnish with watercress.

serves 3–4

Moroccan Chicken with Couscous

PREPARATION 3 hrs 10 mins   COOKING 6–7 mins

4 chicken breast fillets, about
7 oz/200g each, skin off, boned

MARINADE

2 tablespoons olive oil

1 tablespoon finely chopped
fresh parsley

1 teaspoon Moroccan
seasoning

2 tablespoons finely chopped
fresh cilantro

2 teaspoons lemon zest,
finely grated

2 tablespoons lemon juice

salt and pepper to taste

COUSCOUS

1½ cups instant couscous

1½ cups boiling water

2 tablespoons pine nuts,
toasted

⅓ cup seedless golden raisins

1 firm tomato, skinned,
seeded and diced

1 tablespoon butter

1 cup chopped fresh cilantro

PREPARATION

1 Cut 2–3 slashes in each chicken breast,
and place in a non-metallic dish. Combine
marinade ingredients, pour over chicken and
turn to coat both sides. Rub marinade into
the slashes. Cover and marinate 3–4 hours in
refrigerator, turning chicken twice.

2 While chicken is marinating, place couscous,
boiling water and salt in a bowl. Stand until
all water is absorbed. Spoon couscous into a
steamer. place over boiling water and steam
for 30 minutes, forking through occasionally.
Add pine nuts, raisins and butter.

AT THE BARBECUE

1 Prepare barbecue for direct-heat
cooking, medium heat. Place steamer at the
side of grill to keep hot. Oil the grill bars or
plate well. Place chicken top side down and
cook for 2 minutes. Turn, then press spoonfuls
of solid part of marinade on top. Cook for
2–3 minutes more or until cooked through.

2 Mix the cilantro through the couscous,
then spoon the couscous onto serving
platter. Carve the chicken into thick slices,
then place overlapping slices on top of
couscous. Serve immediately.

Teriyaki Chicken Drummettes

serves 4

PREPARATION 3 hrs   COOKING 10–12 mins

20 chicken drummettes

½ cup Teriyaki sauce
(see page 186)

2 zucchini

2 heads broccoli

2 bunches bok choy

PREPARATION

1 Place the chicken drummettes in a shallow dish. Pour over the marinade, then place in the refrigerator for 3 hours.

2 Prepare the vegetables. Wash and slice the zucchini on the diagonal ¾ in/15mm thick, wash, then cut the broccoli into small pieces. Remove the large outer leaves of the bokchoy and wash under running water. Do not shake off the excess water, which will help the cooking process.

AT THE BARBECUE

1 Prepare the barbecue for direct-heat cooking. Oil the grill well. Place on the marinated drummettes. Cook, turning regularly, for 10–12 minutes. At the same time, place on the vegetables and brush with extra marinade. Remove once the vegetables are crisp and tender. Serve on a dinner plate, placing the chicken drummettes in a pile on top of the vegetables.

Barbecued Oysters in Chili Sauce

serves 3-4

PREPARATION 6 mins   COOKING 11–12 mins

12 fresh oysters in half shell

1 tablespoon unsalted butter

½ teaspoon crushed garlic

2 tablespoons fresh lemon juice

2 tablespoons chili sauce of choice

TO GARNISH

zest of lemon

chili flakes

PREPARATION

1 Melt the butter in a small pan. Add the garlic and cook just until the butter colors. Remove from heat and add the lemon juice and chili sauce. Stir to combine.

2 Prepare a metal tray (a Swiss roll tin, for example) with a layer of cooking salt about ½ in/1cm deep. Take sauce, tray and oysters to the barbecue.

AT THE BARBECUE

1 Place the tray of salt on grill over direct high heat. When salt has heated well, remove to the side. Stand the oysters in their shell in the tray, pushing shells into the salt to prevent them tipping. Using a teaspoon, spoon sauce over each oyster. Place the tray on the grill and cook 5–6 minutes or until sauce around the oyster bubbles. Remove immediately and serve garnished with lemon zest and chili flakes.

Lemon Pepper Swordfish Steaks

serves 4

Lemon Pepper
Swordfish Steaks

PREPARATION 30 mins   COOKING 6–8 mins

4 oz/125g unsalted butter, softened

1 teaspoon freshly crushed garlic

2 tablespoons finely chopped fresh basil

4 swordfish steaks

1 tablespoon olive oil

2 teaspoons lemon pepper

1 red pepper, quartered

1 yellow pepper, quartered

4 zucchini, sliced lengthwise

PREPARATION

1 Mix the butter, garlic and basil together. Pile into a butter pot and refrigerate.Brush the swordfish steaks on both sides with oil and sprinkle with the lemon pepper. Cover and stand 20 minutes before cooking.

2 Prepare vegetables. Brush both sides with oil. Take all to the barbecue area including butter pot.

AT THE BARBECUE

1 Prepare barbecue for direct-heat cooking and heat to high. Oil the grill plate well. Oil the vegetables once more, place onto the grill furthest away from you. Oil the fish once more and place at front of the grill. Cook for 2–3 minutes each side. They may need a little longer, depending on thickness. Turn fish and vegetables. Fish is cooked when it flakes easily when fork tested.

2 Remove vegetables to heated plates and sit fish on top. Top the fish with a good dollop of basil butter and serve immediately with hot bread and a side salad.

Salmon Cutlets with Thai Seasoning

serves 4

Salmon Cutlets with Thai Seasoning

PREPARATION 35 mins   COOKING 7 mins

1½ cups jasmine rice, steamed

1 cup toasted sesame seeds

4 salmon cutlets

2 teaspoons oil

6 tablespoons Thai seasoning

4 scallions, trimmed

¾ cup Thai marinade

(see page 183)

PREPARATION

1 Steam the rice, mix through the sesame seeds and place in a container suitable for reheating.

2 Rub the salmon with oil and sprinkle with seasoning, both sides. Cover and set aside for 20 minutes.

3 Cut the scallions diagonally into 1 in/25mm lengths, including some of the green part. Place onto 2 foil squares, drizzle with a little marinade and form into a parcel with a double fold top and sides. Take all to the barbecue area.

AT THE BARBECUE

1 Prepare barbecue for direct-heat grilling and heat to hot. Place the steamed rice at edge of the grill to keep hot.

2 Oil the grill well. Place on the salmon and cook 2 minutes. Turn salmon and parcel and cook 2 minutes more. Remove parcel. Brush top of salmon with marinade, turn and cook 1 minute. Repeat and cook until done when tested. Divide the onions between 4 plates place on top a mound of rice and the glazed salmon. Serve immediately.

Barbecued Lobster Tails with Tropical Salsa

Barbecued Lobster Tails with Tropical Salsa

PREPARATION 15–20 mins   COOKING 7–10 mins

4 green (raw) lobster tails

3 oz/90g softened butter

2 teaspoons freshly crushed garlic

1 teaspoon lemon pepper

2 tablespoons finely chopped fresh cilantro

lime cut into wedges

TROPICAL SALSA

1 large avocado

juice of 1 lemon

2 Lebanese cucumbers

1 mango

2 tablespoons red onion, finely chopped

¼ cup sweet chili sauce

PREPARATION

1 To prepare the salsa, peel and cut avocado, cucumbers and mango into ½ in/1cm cubes. Then drizzle with lemon juice. Toss together with chopped onion and chili sauce. Cover and refrigerate until needed.

2 With kitchen scissors, cut each side of the soft shell of the underside of the lobster tails and remove. Run a metal skewer through the length of each tail to keep them flat while cooking. Soften the butter and mix the garlic, lemon pepper and cilantro together. Spread a coating on the lobster meat. Take all to the barbecue area.

AT THE BARBECUE

1 Prepare barbecue for direct-heat cooking, heat to high. Oil the grill bars well. Place the lobster tails cut side down and cook for 2 minutes to sear the meat. Turn over to shell side down and cook 5–8 minutes until the shell turns red and the meat is white and firm but not dry. Brush the meat twice with butter at intervals. While lobsters are cooking place the lime wedges on the grill to color a little. Brush with chili sauce.

2 Remove the lobsters to a platter, place a dob of butter on top, garnish with grilled lime wedges and serve with salsa.

Shrimp and Scallop Skewers

serves 6

Shrimp and Scallop Skewers

PREPARATION 45 mins COOKING 4–6 mins

2 lb/1kg medium-size green jumbo shrimps

12 scallops

1 red onion, cut in wedges

2 tablespoons melted butter

6 tablespoons sweet chili sauce

1 lb/500g white rice and wild rice mix

12 metal or soaked bamboo skewers

fresh cilantro leaves

PREPARATION

1 Remove the shrimps heads but leave the tails on. Peel and devein the shrimp. Thread 2–3 shrimps, 1 wedge of onion and scallops alternately onto each skewer. Brush with melted butter.

2 Prepare the rice according to packet instructions. Place in heatproof dish suitable for reheating on the barbecue.

AT THE BARBECUE

1 Prepare barbecue for direct-heat cooking, heat to hot and oil the grill bars well. Place the bowl of rice at side of grill to heat. Place on the skewers and cook 2–3 minutes each side, brushing with chili sauce as they cook. If charring occurs place a sheet of baking paper onto the grill, transfer the skewers over and continue to cook until done.

2 Spread the wild rice mixture on a platter and set the skewers on top. Garnish with cilantro leaves. Serve immediately.

Chermoula Sardines

Chermoula Sardines

PREPARATION 2 hrs 10 mins   COOKING 4–5 mins

1 lb/500g fresh sardines

CHERMOULA

1 teaspoon sweet paprika

1 teaspoon ground cumin

1 teaspoon ground cilantro

4 cloves garlic, minced

3 bird's-eye chilies, deseeded and finely chopped

½ bunch cilantro leaves and stems, coarsely chopped

½ bunch mint leaves, coarsely chopped

juice of ½ medium lemon

1 French shallot

1½ tablespoons olive oil

SALSA

2 cartons small cherry tomatoes, quartered

1 small red onion, chopped

1 Lebanese cucumber, diced

reserved chermoula

1 tablespoon olive oil

PREPARATION

1 To prepare the chermoula, place all the ingredients except olive oil into blender and blitz into a paste, adding the olive oil slowly.

2 Place sardines, skin down, in a flat, wide, non-metallic dish. Reserve ⅓ cup of the chermoula and pour remainder over the sardines to cover. Cover and refrigerate for several hours or overnight.

3 To prepare the salsa, toss the tomato, onion and cucumber together in a bowl, then add reserved chermoula and oil. Toss through to combine. Refrigerate.

AT THE BARBECUE

1 Prepare the barbecue for direct-heat cooking. Heat to medium-high and oil the grill bars or plate. Place on the sardines in neat rows, cut-side down, and cook for 2 minutes. Turn and cook for 1–2 minutes or until cooked through. To keep sardines moist as they cook, brush with chermoula marinade from dish.

2 To serve, place a portion of salsa on a hot plate and top with criss-crossed sardines.

Barbecued Fish Pide Burger

Barbecued
Fish Pide Burger

PREPARATION 5 mins   COOKING 10 mins

4 blue-eye cod fillets
(approximately 4 oz/125g each)

4 tablespoons Thai style
seafood seasoning

4 round Turkish pide

3 oz/90g butter, softened

7 oz/200g green salad mix or
shredded lettuce

4 tablespoon sweet chili
sauce of choice

2 large tomatoes, sliced

8 oz/225g traditional tartare
sauce

2 tablespoons finely chopped
scallions

dill sprigs to garnish

PREPARATION

1 Place fish fillets on a plate. Sprinkle both sides with seasoning.Cut the pide in half. Spread lightly with the butter. Prepare the filling ingredients. Take all to the barbecue area.

AT THE BARBECUE

1 Prepare barbecue for direct-heat cooking. Heat to medium-high heat. Grease the grill bars well. Brush the fish with oil, place on the grill bars and cook 3 minutes each side or until cooked through.

2 Place pide, crust side down, to heat a little, turn butter side down to lightly toast.

3 To assemble, place lettuce on base of each portion of pide bread, drizzle very lightly with the chili sauce if desired. Top with 3 tomato slices. Place on the grilled fish, top with tartare sauce and sprinkle with chopped scallion. Place on the top pide.

Oregano Cod Fillets

serves 3

Oregano Cod Fillets

PREPARATION 22 mins   COOKING 9–12 mins

3–4 cod fillets

oregano seasoning

1 teaspoon freshly chopped

chili

1 tablespoon olive oil

HOT CHUTNEY SALAD

1 red and 1 green pepper,

halved lengthwise, seeds and

veins removed and sliced

¼ in/5mm wide

3 medium tomatoes,

quartered then halved

8 oz/250g green tomato relish

(see page 167)

12 black olives, pitted

PREPARATION

1 Sprinkle the oregano seasoning on both sides of the fillets. Stand for 20 minutes. Mix the chili and oil together. Set aside.

2 Place sliced red and green peppers and cut tomatoes in a heatproof bowl. Take cod, chili, oil and salad ingredients to the barbecue.

AT THE BARBECUE

1 Prepare barbecue for direct-heat cooking. Oil the grill plate well. Place pepper strips and tomatoes on plate, toss for 2–3 minutes to cook, slightly retaining crunch. Return to heatproof bowl. Stir in sufficient relish to form a good mix and add the olives. Stand at side of barbecue to keep warm.

2 Oil the clean part of grill plate. Brush the fish fillets with chili oil, place on plate and cook 3–4 minutes each side, brushing with the oil as it cooks.

3 Place a bed of hot salad on plates and place a cod fillet on top. Serve immediately.

Whole Barbecued Snapper

serves 8-10

Whole Barbecued Snapper

PREPARATION 5 mins   COOKING 50–55 mins

3-4 lb/1.5-2kg whole snapper, scaled and cleaned

1 bunch fresh dill, rinsed

175g Thai marinade
(see page 183)

1 large sheet heavy duty foil, well oiled

PREPARATION

1 Rinse snapper cavity and pat dry with paper towels. Brush inside cavity with marinade. Place the foil sheet on work surface, oiled side up. Spread the dill in the centre where fish will sit, retaining 3 stalks for the top and sit the fish on top. Brush the top of snapper with Thai marinade and place reserved dill on top. Lift the foil to meet in the centre, make a double fold to seal, leaving air space. Double fold the ends.

AT THE BARBECUE

1 Prepare barbecue for indirect-heat cooking and heat to medium high. Place foil package over indirect heat and cook for 45–50 minutes according to weight, without turning. To test, carefully unfold foil and place a knife or skewer in the cavity. If fish lifts easily off the bones, it is cooked.

2 Remove in foil to a platter, stand 5 minutes. Fold back the foil from around the fish and serve with suitable accompaniments.

Chili Honeyed Whiting

serves 4

Chili Honeyed Whiting

PREPARATION 1 hr 10 mins   COOKING 8–10 mins

2 whole whiting (1–1¼ lb/
500–650g each)

MARINADE

1 tablespoon olive oil

1 medium red onion, finely
diced

1 tablespoon finely chopped
fresh parsley

1 teaspoon chopped chives

⅓ cup honey

1 tablespoon soy sauce

1 teaspoon chili flakes

PREPARATION

1   Using kitchen scissors, cut the fins off the fish and trim the tail to a V shape. Make 3 parallel slashes on both sides of the fish, holding knife at an angle.

2   Mix the marinade ingredients together in a bowl, then spoon some of it into the cavity of each fish. Spoon remainder into the slashes and over top. Cover and refrigerate 1 hour. Place securely in a well-oiled fish rack. Take fish to barbecue area.

AT THE BARBECUE

1   Prepare the barbecue for direct-heat cooking, heat to high. Place the naked fish on the hot grill bars and cook 4–5 minutes each side, depending on size. Serve immediately with salad of choice.

Grilled Sumac Catfish

PREPARATION 10 mins   COOKING 16–20 mins

4 catfish (1–1¼ lb/

500–600g each)

2 tablespoons sumac spice

4 tablespoons olive oil

bunch of fresh dill

2 lemons

4 serves of mixed

Mediterranean vegetables

(see page 155)

8–12 wooden skewers, soaked

for 30 minutes

PREPARATION

1 Ask the fish monger to clean and gut the fish and remove the head. Cut off the fins and trim the tail with a pair of kitchen scissors. In a small bowl mix together the olive oil and the sumac. Slice the lemons. Wash the dill and trim off the stalks.

2 Place the fish on their backs on a chopping board. Into each fish cavity place a good handful of dill and 2–3 slices of lemon, then pour on some of the oil and sumac mix. With 2–3 small wooden skewers, fasten together the fish so dill and lemon do not fall out during cooking.

3 Turn the fish over and rub the oil and sumac mix well into the fish.

AT THE BARBECUE

1 Prepare the barbecue for direct-heat cooking. Oil the grill bars well. Cook the fish on each side for 8–10 minutes. To serve, place the mixed Mediterranean vegetables onto a plate and place the flathead on top.

Chat Potatoes with Tomato Relish

serves 4

PREPARATION 6 mins   COOKING 20 mins

10 oz/300g medium-sized chat potatoes, washed

1 tablespoon oil

1 teaspoon salt

½ cup chunky tomato relish (see page 181)

PREPARATION

1 Place the washed potatoes in a bowl. Combine oil and salt, pour over potatoes and toss to coat. Wrap each potato in a piece of foil.

AT THE BARBECUE

1 Place potatoes on the barbecue grill or hot plate as soon as you light the barbecue. The potatoes will heat and get a head start before it is hot enough to cook the meat. Turn the potatoes at times. When barbecue heats up, turn potatoes more frequently.

2 Test with skewer. If soft, remove and keep warm. Potatoes will take about 20 minutes with the slow start. Fold foil back from potatoes. Cut a cross in the top and squeeze from the base to open out. Squeeze a good dollop of relish into centre of potato and serve immediately.

Garlic and Herb Breads

Garlic and Herb Breads

PREPARATION 10 mins   **COOKING** 10 mins

1 long bread stick or 2 panini

3 oz/90g flavored butter (see below)

PESTO BUTTER

3 oz/90g butter, softened

small bunch basil, finely chopped

2 tablespoons grated Parmesan cheese

LEMON PEPPER BUTTER

3 oz/90g butter

1 tablespoon lemon juice

2 tablespoons lemon pepper

MUSTARD BUTTER

3 oz/90g butter

1 tablespoon Dijonaise

PREPARATION

1 Cut the bread diagonally into ½ in/1cm-thick pieces. Lightly spread each cut surface with a brush of oil.

PESTO BUTTER

Mix softened butter, chopped basil and Parmesan together until smooth.

LEMON PEPPER BUTTER

Mix softened butter, lemon juice and lemon pepper together until smooth.

MUSTARD BUTTER

Mix softened butter and mustard until smooth.

AT THE BARBECUE

1 Place bread slices on the barbecue grill bars or plate (at the side of other foods cooking). Cook for 1–2 minutes per side until grill line appears. Serve warm breads immediately with small dishes of each flavored butter so that your guests can choose their toppings.

Garlic and Herbed Damper

serves 4

Garlic and Herbed Damper

PREPARATION 15 mins   COOKING 25–30 mins

3 cups all-purpose flour

3 teaspoons baking powder

½ teaspoon salt

1 teaspoon freshly chopped

garlic

1 teaspoon fresh oregano,

finely chopped

1 tablespoon finely chopped

fresh basil

1 tablespoon finely chopped

fresh parsley

1½ cups milk

2 tablespoons oil

milk for glazing

PREPARATION

1 Sift flour, salt and baking powder into a large mixing bowl and make a well in the centre. Add garlic, oregano, basil, parsley, milk and oil and stir with a round-bladed knife untill you have a soft, sticky dough. Turn out onto a lightly floured board, dust top with flour and knead lightly with 3–4 turns to smooth a little. Pat into a round and place in a greased 8 in/20cm shallow skillet or flat oven slide. Cut a cross on top with sharp knife and glaze with a little milk.

AT THE BARBECUE

1 Place in barbecue over indirect hot heat, close lid or hood and cook for 25–30 minutes or until golden and sounds hollow when tapped. Serve hot or warm with butter to accompany barbecue meals.

Mixed Asian Vegetables

serves 4

Mixed Asian Vegetables

PREPARATION 8 mins   COOKING 8 mins

1 packet baby corn

1 red pepper

2 bunches bok choy

2 bunches pak choy

2 bunches Chinese broccoli

1 bunch scallions

4 oz/115g snow peas,

strings removed

½ cup honey

1 teaspoon chili paste

2 tablespoon soy sauce

PREPARATION

1 Cut the ends off the baby corn. Slice the pepper into 1 in/25mm strips.Wash and trim the bok choy, pak choy and Chinese broccoli, but do not shake off the excess water as this will help with the cooking. Cut the scallions into 1 in/25mm lengths. Top the snow peas. Combine the honey, chili paste and soy sauce into a marinade and brush over all the vegetables.

AT THE BARBECUE

1 Prepare the barbecue for direct-heat cooking. Oil the grill well. Place the vegetables on the grill. Move them around during cooking and brush with more marinade. Once they are colored and wilted, remove from the heat. Serve on a large platter for the guests to help themselves.

Mixed Mediterranean Vegetables

serves 4

Mixed Mediterranean Vegetables

PREPARATION 8 mins **COOKING** 35 mins

8 squash

2 eggplant

4 zucchini

1 red pepper

1 orange pepper

1 green pepper

2 medium red onions

2 tablespoons fresh oregano

2 tablespoons finely chopped fresh basil

2 tablespoons finely chopped fresh parsley

6 tablespoons olive oil

PREPARATION

1 Cut the squash into quarters. Slice the eggplant into ¾ in/15mm thickness. Slice zucchini on the diagonal into ¾ in/15mm thickness. Peel the red onion. Leave the root attached, and cut into eighths.

2 Place prepared vegetables in a bowl. Mix herbs and oil together, pour over vegetables and toss.

AT THE BARBECUE

1 Prepare the barbecue for direct cooking. Oil all three peppers and place on the grill. Turn them when they start to blister and burn. Once the whole pepper is blistered, remove from the grill and place into a bowl cover with plastic wrap. This will make the pepper sweat and easier to peel.

2 Skin the peppers, cut into 1 in/25mm wide strips. Place into the bowl of vegetables.Re-oil the grill, tip the contents of the bowl onto the grill. Cook while tossing until crisp, tender and lightly charred. Serve on a large platter for the guests to help themselves.

Green Vegetable Barbecue

serves 6–8

Green Vegetable Barbecue

PREPARATION 25–30 mins   COOKING 5 mins

⅓ cup olive oil

⅓ teaspoon chili flakes

5 oz/150g broccoli, cut into small florets

2–3 zucchini, halved lengthwise and cut into ½ in/1cm slices

5 oz/150g snow peas, topped and strings removed

PREPARATION

1 Mix the oil and chili flakes together and stand 20 minutes. Prepare vegetables. Mix together in a bowl. Pour in the chili oil and toss to coat the vegetables.

AT THE BARBECUE

1 Oil the hot barbecue grill plate over a large area and tip on the vegetables. Spread out a little, then commence to toss at short intervals with wide spatulas, lifting from underneath the pile and turning over. Continue to cook in this fashion until vegetables are crisp and tender. Sprinkle with chili flakes. Remove to a serving dish. Serve immediately.

Garlic and Cheese Kipflers

serves 4

Garlic and Cheese Kipflers

PREPARATION 6 mins   COOKING 22 mins

2 lb/1kg medium sized Kipfler potatoes, scrubbed

1 teaspoon freshly crushed garlic

2 tablespoons butter, softened

1½ cups mozzarella cheese, finely grated

1 Wrap potatoes in foil and cook as for chat potatoes with tomato relish (see page 147). Mix garlic and butter together.

2 When ready turn back the foil to half way down. Cut each potato lengthwise across centre of top with out cutting through. Open out the potato. Add a dob of garlic butter, spread along crease as it melts. Sprinkle a little cheese on top. Place on a platter, cover with foil. Stored heat will melt cheese quickly. Otherwise, place potatoes on barbecue with hood down to melt the cheese. Serve immediately.

serves 4

Eggplant and Zucchini Salsa Stack

PREPARATION 4 mins   COOKING 6–8 mins

2–3 medium-sized eggplants

2 medium-sized zucchini

½ cup olive oil

1 teaspoon freshly crushed garlic

1 cup chunky salsa

1 packet Cheddar cheese slices cut into ¾ in/15mm strips

PREPARATION

1 Slice eggplant and zucchini crosswise into ¾ in/15mm thick slices. Mix oil and garlic together and brush both sides of eggplant slices.

AT THE BARBECUE

1 Prepare barbecue for direct-heat cooking. Oil the grill well and place vegetables on hot barbecue grill bars. Cook for 3–4 minutes each side until rosy brown. Put the salsa in a heatproof bowl on the barbecue.

2 As eggplant cooks, stack on a tray and spread with cheese. Stand tray with lid down in covered barbecue to melt the cheese, if possible for 30 seconds.

3 Remove from barbecue and top with warmed salsa. Serve on a plater. Serve with garlic and herb breads (see page 149) or garlic and herbed damper (see page 151).

Lemon Potato Wedges

Lemon Potato Wedges

PREPARATION 5 mins   COOKING 20 mins

4–6 medium-sized potatoes, peeled

1 teaspoon freshly crushed garlic

3 tablespoons olive oil

½ cup water

½ teaspoon lemon pepper

⅓ cup fresh lemon juice

salt

PREPARATION

1 Halve the potatoes then cut each half into 4–6 wedges. Place into a large bowl. Mix garlic, oil, water and lemon juice together, pour over potatoes and toss well to coat. Place in a shallow baking dish in a single layer and sprinkle with lemon pepper.

AT THE BARBECUE

1 Cook over direct heat in a covered barbecue. Cook for 20 minutes. Turn after 10 minutes. If drying out, add water continue to cook and turn until tender and crisp. Can be moved to indirect heat while other dishes finish cooking. To serve, sprinkle lightly with salt.

Hotcakes with Horseradish and Relish

Hotcakes with Horseradish and Relish

PREPARATION 8 mins   **COOKING** 15 mins

HOTCAKES

1 cup all-purpose flour

1 teaspoon baking powder

pinch salt

1 cup milk

1 egg

1 teaspoon horseradish cream

½ teaspoon basil leaves

TOPPINGS

barbecue relish (see page 173)

green tomato relish

(see page 167)

corn relish (see page 184)

PREPARATION

1 Sift flour, baking powder and salt together in a bowl. Beat together the milk, egg, horseradish cream and basil leaves. Pour into the flour and lightly stir until a smooth batter is formed.

AT THE BARBECUE

1 Grease the hot barbecue grill plate well. Drop a tablespoon of batter onto the hot plate from the tip end of a spoon. Work quickly, leaving a space between each for spreading. Turn when bubbles begin to break on surface and cook other side. Lift to a cloth-lined tray as they cook and cover to keep warm. To serve, top with a spoonful of pickle or relish of choice.

serves 4 | # Cajun Chat Potatoes

PREPARATION 5 mins   COOKING 20–25 mins

1 lb/500g **chat potatoes**
4 tablespoons **olive** oil
2 tablespoons **Cajun** spice mix
2 teaspoons **salt**

PREPARATION

1 Wash the potatoes well. Cut the potatoes in half. In a large bowl place the potatoes, olive oil, Cajun spice mix and salt. Toss to coat thoroughly. Place the potatoes into a baking dish and cover with foil.

AT THE BARBECUE

1 Place the dish onto grill plate and cover or pull down barbecue lid. Check potatoes to make sure they don't stick to the bottom of the dish. The potatoes will take 20–25 minutes to cook. Test with a skewer.

We are proud to present the **COLLECTORS EDITION**
series of books as a suite of our favourite
and most asked for recipes.

This series is bound together in a
premium collectable format that can be added
to the recipe section of your bookshelf.

Watch out for the following titles, start collecting,
continue cooking, and finally, enjoy the end results
of a beautifully prepared meal.

COLLECTORS EDITIONS

makes 2 cups | # Green Tomato Relish

PREPARATION 5 mins   COOKING 32–40 mins

1 onion, grated	¼ cup malt vinegar
1 teaspoon freshly crushed garlic	⅓ cup water

1 onion, grated

1 teaspoon freshly crushed garlic

3 medium green tomatoes, diced into medium-size pieces

2 tablespoons olive oil

1 green apple, skinned and cored, then grated

3 tablespoons corn syrup

1 teaspoon ground cumin

¼ teaspoon curry powder

½ teaspoon white pepper

2 teaspoons salt

2 teaspoons cornstarch

¼ cup malt vinegar

⅓ cup water

1 Fry the onion, garlic and tomato in the olive oil for 6–7 minutes, stirring constantly. Add all other ingredients and stir to combine. Simmer for 25 minutes, stirring occasionally.

2 Allow to cool and transfer to an airtight container. Makes approximately 2 cups in finished volume. Can be stored in the refrigerator for approximately 8 weeks.

Apricot Marinade

makes 2 cups

Apricot Marinade

PREPARATION 2 mins   **COOKING** 11 mins

1 onion, grated

2 tablespoons olive oil

½ teaspoon ground ginger

1½ cups puréed apricot conserve

1 teaspoon soy sauce

½ cup dry sherry

½ cup water

juice of 1 lemon

1 Sauté onion in olive oil for 3 minutes, add ground ginger and fry for a further 2 minutes. Add all other ingredients except lemon juice. Mix together thoroughly. Heat sauce and simmer for 5 minutes. Add lemon juice and stir through.

2 Allow to cool, then transfer to an airtight container. Makes approximately 2 cups in finished volume. Can be stored in the refrigerator for approximately 4 weeks.

Chinese Beef Stir-Fry Sauce

makes 2 cups

Chinese Beef Stir-Fry Sauce

PREPARATION 2 mins   COOKING 13 mins

4 teaspoons freshly crushed garlic

4 teaspoons sesame oil

3 tablespoons plum conserve

4 tablespoons honey

¼ cup soy sauce

¼ cup sherry

2 tablespoons tomato sauce

½ cup water

1   Gently fry garlic in sesame oil for 1 minute, stirring constantly. Add all other ingredients.

2   Stir until fully combined, then simmer on a low heat for 10 minutes.

3   Allow to cool, then transfer to an airtight container. Makes approximately 2 cups in finished volume. Can be stored in the refrigerator for approximately 4 weeks.

makes 2 cups

Barbecue Relish

PREPARATION 25 mins   COOKING 25 mins

1 tablespoon vegetable oil

1 onion, grated

2 teaspoons freshly crushed garlic

14 oz/400g canned crushed tomatoes

2 tablespoons corn syrup

¼ cup tomato ketchup

2 teaspoons balsamic vinegar

2 tablespoons Worcestershire sauce

¼ cup golden raisins, roughly chopped

zest of 1 lemon

zest of 1 orange

1 red pepper, roasted, deseeded, skin removed and diced

1 teaspoon salt

1 Add the vegetable oil to a saucepan and gently fry the onion for about 2–3 minutes or until translucent. Add the garlic and fry for 1 more minute. Add all other ingredients, liquid ingredients first.

2 Stir until fully combined and simmer on a low heat for 20 minutes. Allow to cool, then transfer to an airtight container. Makes approximately 2 cups in finished volume. Can be stored in the refrigerator for approximately 4 weeks.

Mango Chutney

Mango Chutney

PREPARATION 40 mins   **COOKING** 25–26 mins

1 tablespoon vegetable oil

⅔ onion, grated

1 teaspoon freshly crushed garlic

½ cup water

¼ teaspoon Worcestershire sauce

2 tablespoons honey

1 mango, flesh removed from pip and skin, then diced

2 red peppers, roasted, deseeded, skin removed, and diced

¼ cup golden raisins

½ green apple, peeled, cored and diced

1 small red chili, cut in half lengthwise

1 cinnamon stick

¼ teaspoon sweet paprika

¼ teaspoon allspice

1 teaspoon salt

1 Add the vegetable oil to a saucepan and gently fry the onion for about 2–3 minutes or until translucent. Add the garlic and fry for 1 more minute. Add all other ingredients, liquid ingredients first.

2 Stir until fully combined, then simmer on a low heat for 20 minutes. Allow to cool, then transfer to an airtight container. Makes approximately 2 cups in finished volume. Can be stored in the refrigerator for approximately 4 weeks.

Caramelised Onion and Red Wine Reduction

makes 2 cups

PREPARATION 3 mins   COOKING 17–23 mins

2 tablespoons olive oil

1 onion, puréed

2 teaspoons crushed garlic

2 tablespoons butter

½ teaspoon salt

½ teaspoon white pepper

4 fresh bay leaves

½ cup dry red wine

1 teaspoon balsamic vinegar

¼ teaspoon sweet paprika

1 teaspoon honey

1 tablespoon brown sugar

1 Add the olive oil to a skillet and gently fry the onion, stirring regularly for about 15–20 minutes until medium brown. Add the garlic and gently fry for 2–3 more minutes. Add all other ingredients and stir to combine.

2 Allow to cool, then transfer to an airtight container. Makes approximately 2 cups in finished volume. Can be stored in the refrigerator for approximately 2 weeks.

| Satay Marinade

PREPARATION 4 mins   COOKING 16–17 mins

½ teaspoon ground ginger

½ teaspoon ground cilantro

¼ teaspoon ground cumin

½ onion, grated

2 tablespoons peanut oil

1 teaspoon freshly crushed garlic

¾ cup roasted peanuts, puréed into a paste

2 teaspoons tomato paste

⅔ cup creamed coconut

3 tablespoons honey

¼ teaspoon salt

1   Tip all the spices into a dry skillet and fry gently, stirring constantly until they begin to smoke. Remove from the heat and continue to stir for another minute. Add grated onion and quickly combine.

2   Return to the heat and add the peanut oil. Gently fry spices and onion for 3–4 minutes, then add garlic. Fry for 1 minute, then add all other ingredients. Simmer for 10 minutes.

3   Allow to cool, then transfer to an airtight container. Makes approximately 2 cups in finished volume. Can be stored in the refrigerator for approximately 1 week.

Fruit Chutney

PREPARATION 10 mins   **COOKING** 22 mins

2 tablespoons olive oil

1½ cups water

1 onion, grated

2 green apples, skinned and cored, then grated

½ cup dried apricots, finely diced

½ cup golden raisins

zest of 1 orange

flesh of 1 orange, cut into small pieces

2 heaped tablespoons brown sugar

½ teaspoon chili paste

¼ teaspoon ground turmeric

½ teaspoon salt

½ teaspoon freshly ground black pepper

1 bay leaf

3 cloves

3 tablespoons Worcestershire sauce

½ cup kecap manis

2 teaspoons cornstarch

1 Pour olive oil into saucepan. Add 1 cup of the water and the onion and fry for 2 minutes, stirring occasionally. Add all other ingredients to the pot except the cornstarch, combine thoroughly.

2 Add a little of the remaining water to the cornstarch and work into a paste. Add the rest of the water to the cornstarch, and then add the mixture to the pot. Stir all ingredients together and simmer on low heat for 15 minutes.

3 Allow to cool, then transfer to an airtight container. Makes approximately 2 cups in finished volume. Can be stored in the refrigerator for approximately 6–8 weeks.

Chunky Tomato Relish

makes 2 cups

Chunky Tomato Relish

PREPARATION 30 mins **COOKING** 23–24 mins

2 tablespoons olive oil

1 onion, grated

2 teaspoons freshly crushed garlic

14 oz/400g canned chopped tomatoes

1 tablespoon Worcestershire sauce

1 tablespoon tomato paste

¼ cup corn syrup

8 dill pickles, medium diced

1 red pepper, roasted, deseeded, skin removed, and diced

½ teaspoon freshly ground black pepper

¼ teaspoon allspice

¼ teaspoon sweet paprika

2 fresh bay leaves

1 teaspoon Dijon mustard

1 teaspoon salt

1 cup water

1 Add the olive oil to a saucepan and gently fry the onion for about 2–3 minutes until translucent. Add the garlic and fry for 1 more minute.

2 Add tomatoes, Worcestershire sauce, tomato paste and stir until all combined. Simmer for 5 minutes, then add all other ingredients. Simmer for a further 15 minutes.

3 Allow to cool, then transfer to an airtight container. Makes approximately 2 cups in finished volume. Can be stored in the refrigerator for approximately 6 weeks.

Thai Marinade

Thai Marinade

PREPARATION 35 mins   **COOKING** 18 mins

1 teaspoon sesame oil

1 teaspoon chili oil

1 teaspoon peanut oil

1 onion, grated

2 teaspoons freshly minced garlic

2 teaspoons freshly minced ginger

2 red peppers, roasted, deseeded, skin removed and finely diced

1 whole lime, puréed

2 teaspoons light soy sauce

1 tablespoon freshly ground black pepper

4 tablespoons brown sugar

1 red chili, cut lengthwise

1½ cups water

1 teaspoon cornstarch

1 small bunch cilantro leaves, stalks removed and finely chopped

1   Pour all oils into a saucepan. Add onion and fry for 2 minutes, stirring occasionally. Add garlic and ginger and continue to fry for 2 more minutes.

2   Add all other ingredients except water, cornstarch and cilantro. Stir ingredients thoroughly. Add a little of the water to the cornstarch and work into a paste.

3   Add the rest of the water to the cornstarch, and then add the mixture to the pot. Stir to combine and simmer for 10 minutes. Add cilantro and cook for another 2 minutes.

4   Allow to cool. Remove the 2 chili pieces and transfer marinade to an airtight container. Makes approximately 2½ cups in finished volume. Can be stored in the refrigerator for approximately 6–8 weeks.

| # Corn Relish

PREPARATION 28 mins   COOKING 20 mins

2 tablespoons yellow mustard seeds

1 cup water

2 teaspoons cornstarch

1 Add onion to oil in a saucepan and fry for 2 minutes, stirring occasionally. Add celery and pepper and continue to fry for 2 more minutes. Add all other ingredients except water and cornstarch and stir thoroughly.

2 Add a little of the water to the cornstarch and work into a paste. Add the rest of the water to the cornstarch, and then add the mixture to the pot.

3 Stir to combine and simmer for 15 minutes. Allow to cool, then transfer to an airtight container. Makes approximately 2½ cups in finished volume. Can be stored in the refrigerator for 2 weeks.

1 onion, grated

2 tablespoons olive oil

2 sticks celery, finely diced

¼ red pepper, deseeded and finely diced

14 oz/400g can corn, coarsely puréed

1 teaspoon freshly crushed garlic

1 teaspoon salt

2 teaspoons sugar

½ teaspoon ground white pepper

¼ teaspoon Worcestershire sauce

1 tablespoon corn syrup

2 teaspoons white vinegar

Tomato and Chili Pickle

PREPARATION 30 mins   COOKING 22 mins

1 Pour olive oil into a saucepan. Add onion and fry for 2 minutes, stirring occasionally. Add all other ingredients except cornstarch and water and combine thoroughly.

2 Add a little of the water to the cornstarch and work into a paste. Add the rest of the water to the cornstarch, and then add the mixture to the pot. Stir all ingredients together and simmer on low heat for 20 minutes.

3 Allow to cool, then transfer to an airtight container. Makes approximately 2 cups in finished volume. Can be stored in the refrigerator for approximately 6 weeks.

2 tablespoons olive oil

2 small onions, grated

14 oz/400g canned crushed tomatoes

1½ red peppers, roasted, deseeded, skin removed, and finely diced

6 dill pickles, finely diced

1¼ tablespoons chili paste

2 tablespoons honey

2 teaspoons sweet paprika

1 tablespoon yellow mustard seeds

1 tablespoon salt

1 teaspoon freshly ground black pepper

1 teaspoon cornstarch

⅓ cup water

makes 1 cup | Teriyaki Sauce

PREPARATION 6 mins   **COOKING** 10 mins

½ cup kecap manis

1 cup water

4 tablespoons brown sugar

1½ tablespoons freshly
minced garlic

4 tablespoons freshly
minced ginger

¼ cup honey

1 Combine kecap manis, water, brown sugar, garlic and ginger in a medium-size saucepan.

2 Bring to a boil, add honey and stir constantly. Cook for approximately 8 minutes until sauce thickens slightly.

PREPARATION 3 mins   COOKING 12 mins

1¼ cups plum conserve

¼ cup sugar

1 small red chili, finely

chopped

2 whole star anise

1 tablespoon Worcestershire

sauce

1 teaspoon salt

juice of 1 medium lemon

¾ cup water

2 teaspoons cornstarch

1   Put plum conserve into a skillet. Add all other ingredients except ¼ cup of water and cornstarch. Stir to combine and simmer for 5 minutes

2   Add a little of the water to the cornstarch and work to a paste. Add the rest of the water to the cornstarch and then add to the plum marinade. Stir to combine and simmer for another 5 minutes.

3   Allow to cool. Remove the star anise and transfer the marinade to an airtight container. Makes approximately 2 cups in finished volume. Can be stored in the refrigerator for approximately 6 weeks.

Red Wine and Garlic Marinade

makes 2 cups

Red Wine and Garlic Marinade

PREPARATION 4 mins   **COOKING** 16 mins

1½ cups dry red wine

1 tablespoon chopped fresh thyme

1 teaspoon salt

1 teaspoon freshly ground black pepper

3 tablespoons Worcestershire sauce

2 cloves garlic, finely chopped

3 tablespoons soy sauce

¾ cup water

3 teaspoons cornstarch

1 Put red wine into a saucepan. Add all other ingredients except ¼ cup of water and cornstarch. Stir to combine and simmer for 10 minutes.

2 Add a little of the water to the cornstarch to make a paste. Add the rest of the water to the cornstarch, and then add to the marinade. Stir to combine, and then simmer for a further 5 minutes. Adjust the seasoning.

3 Allow to cool and transfer to an airtight container. Makes approximately 2 cups in finished volume. Can be stored in the refrigerator for approximately 4 weeks.

Index